Big Words

BETH BLAND ENGEL

LODESTAR BOOKS E. P. DUTTON NEW YORK

Library of Congress Cataloging in Publication Data
Engel, Beth Bland, date   Big words.
Summary: Twelve-year-old Sandy befriends a young black
she finds hiding on her father's property after he has
been accused of murdering a white woman in their south
Georgia town in 1965.
[1. Racism—Fiction. 2. United States—Race relations
—Fiction] I. Title.
PZ7.E6997Bi 1982 [Fic] 82-5036
ISBN 0-525-66779-2   AACR2

Published in the United States by E. P. Dutton, Inc.,
2 Park Avenue, New York, N.Y. 10016
Published simultaneously in Canada by Clarke,
Irwin & Company Limited, Toronto and Vancouver
Editor: Virginia Buckley   Designer: Trish Parcell

Printed in the U.S.A.   First Edition

10 9 8 7 6 5 4 3 2 1

for David Bland, then and now,
and for my daughters, Ina Jean and Deborah, with love

It was Saturday afternoon, and I was stretched out, flat on my stomach, around the side of the porch. I wasn't really doing anything but minding my own business and trying to keep the flies away. When the weather turns warm, we get more pesky flies than you can shake a stick at and a big fat May fly was buzzing around my head.

I was trying to make myself study since I have only six more days—six measly little days—to memorize the Gettysburg Address letter-perfect for Commencement Exercises next Friday. I know most of it by heart, but a few of the big words keep tripping me up, and I certainly don't want to get up on that stage and make a fool of myself.

Holding my history book in my hands I examined it cover to cover. It's a big green book, and it's splotched all over and faded some in streaks where I got caught in the rain. On the front it says *History of the United States*. The first page has written on it with a purple felt-tip pen *Cassandra Cason, Hines City, Georgia*. We live a good five miles from town, but that's still my address if you add the R.F.D. And unfortunately that's my name, no matter what. Not even a middle name which would give me something to choose from. *Cassandra* doesn't fit me at all. If my parents had bothered to give it a second thought before they hauled me down to be christened, they surely would have had more sense than to saddle me with a name like that. Parents can sometimes do the dumbest things, for no good reason at all. Once, when I asked, Mama told me the first Cassandra was a prophet in ancient Greece, the daughter of Priam and Hecuba. If my folks ever hoped to make a prophet out of me, they might as well give up. I wouldn't know how to prophesy if my life depended on it. I'm not even sure how to spell it.

I turned the page and in the middle of the next was *Preface*. I've seen the word before, but I don't really know what it means. Papa's only kidding when he says it's for Peter Rabbit Eats Fish, Alligators Catch 'Em. Papa's always teasing me, but he does it in fun. We get along just fine. If the Lord had given me some clay and said, Make a father, I'd have tried my best to come up with one exactly like the one He gave me.

Mama seldom teases. She's not what you would call a weepy woman, but she's got a mile-wide streak of sadness in her. She tries—really tries—to make jokes, but they always come out twisted and heavy-handed. Papa keeps telling her that a sense of humor is as important to people as oil to the feathers of a duck: It keeps you afloat and lets the worst things slide on off. Mama sighs and shakes her head before she answers, "I know, Tom—and I try my best."

I had wasted enough time, so I flipped on over to the page with the Gettysburg Address and removed the Beatles card I was using as a marker. *Four score and seven years ago our fathers brought forth on this continent, a new nation, conceived in liberty*—I swallowed a yawn and kept going—*and dedicated to the proposition that all men are created equal.* Another great big yawn almost cracked my jaw. It's too danged hot to study in May, much less memorize. May's not good for anything much besides fishing. My eyes found the big catalpa tree in the corner of our side yard. The leaves are ragged on the edges and stripped to the stem by the fuzzy catalpa worms, and Mama has threatened a hundred times to get somebody to chop it down, shade or no shade. Papa and I have outtalked her so far because those worms make super fish bait. But knowing Mama, the days of that tree are numbered.

You don't make much noise memorizing, so the ladies on the front of our L-shaped porch had no way of knowing I was anywhere around. Mama and Aunt Edie and Mrs. Dewberry were rocking and talking, and I decided to tune in long enough to find out if their topic for the day was worth my listening to. Most of the time it isn't, unless a person really cares how much lime it takes to crisp up watermelon rind pickles or how to keep a raglan sleeve from puckering. Junk like that.

Mrs. Dewberry is the talkingest woman in Hines County. Papa says her tongue is tied in the middle so she can wag both ends. I think the only reason Mama tolerates her is because the Dewberrys are our nearest neighbors— practically our only neighbors, since not very many people live this far out of town. She's awfully funny looking, too. To begin with, she wears her hair in a knot on top of her head. My brother, Benjie, remarked one time that it looked like a cow flew over. Of course, Mama sent him away from the dinner table for saying it, but even she smiled a little bit. And Mrs. Dewberry wears glasses so thick you can hardly see her eyes, which look like fat brown chinquapins, and her mouth looks like she has just bitten into a green persimmon. She has a funny way of ending her sentences in a squeak. I think it's the false teeth she wears, but maybe she was born like that. She was squeaking now, "Well, it don't seem right to speak ill

3

of the dead, and the Good Lord knows I try to find some good in everybody, for like my dear departed mother always stressed it on me, 'if you can't say something good about a person, it's better not to say anything,' but that woman was nothing but a cheap hussy, and mark my words, there's bound to be a lot of people sayin' that gettin' murdered in her own bathtub is her just reward for her wickedness."

I missed part of what she was saying but that word *murdered* had jumped out at me like a lightning bolt, and I sat up straight to listen. Mrs. Dewberry went barreling on. "The sinful way she carries on with half the men in Hines City every time her husband leaves town on one of his sellin' trips is a shame and disgrace—I mean it *was* a shame and disgrace. I still can't get used to the idea that she's dead and gone. I can just shut my eyes and see her plain as day, sashayin' up Main Street on Saturday with her skirt as tight as a second skin and her cuttin' those eyes at every fellow in sight."

Mama said, "I don't recall much about her, except she was awfully bowlegged."

"Hell, Laura," Aunt Edie snorted, "that woman wasn't bowlegged—she was plain old pleasure bent. A brood sow could run between her legs and she wouldn't lose her balance."

Their laughter came bouncing around the corner of the porch. They were really quite close. It took no effort to hear every word they said now that I was paying attention—eavesdropping, I guess you might call it, and Mama would skin me alive if she caught me, but it's practically the only way I ever learn anything around here, since most of the grown-ups insist on treating me like a child.

"And I'll tell you another thing," Mrs. Dewberry

squeaked, "that was never no God-given complexion she had. There's some who thought she was a good-looker, but I don't go for all that powder and paint myself. To say nothin' of the eye makeup and the bleached out hair. Heaven only knows what she would have been without the Avon lady and the Roux shampoo." I know she hated to, but she paused for breath. "If that nigger boy hadn't been there on the scene, workin' in her yard, and if he hadn't run away as soon as the news got out, and if Sheriff Wiggins and the posse weren't high-tailin' all over lookin' for him—runnin' like that, there ain't no doubt but what he done it—I'd say her husband could've strangled her, and I wouldn't much blame him if he had."

Now it was Mama's turn again. "I find it mighty hard to believe that young Will Brown would have done such a dreadful thing."

I sat up even straighter. The only Will Brown I knew was a senior at Hines City High. He's captain of the football team and president of the student council, so Mama couldn't've meant him. Now she was saying, "I've known Will's family for years—his grandmother used to wash for my mother—and they've always seemed like a quiet, hard-working, good colored family. Not the sort to get into scrapes, and especially not to go around strangling people in their bathtubs. Why, that boy can't be much more than seventeen years old. If I remember correctly, he was born about the same time as Benjie. As a matter of fact, when they were growing up, the two of them used to hunt and fish together."

I had almost forgotten that, but now I remembered the times I'd watch through the window as they came back across the fields, laughing and talking, their canvas jackets stuffed with squirrels or quail. Will never came in our house, but I'd keep on watching him as he headed

5

down the road for home, growing smaller and smaller in the distance. If this is the Will they are talking about, the whole world has gone crazy.

I listened to Mama again. Her voice was low and troubled. "I can't make myself believe that boy would harm a soul."

Aunt Edie took her turn. "Well, Laura, you know how it is. Human nature is human nature and the way that woman used to parade around with shorts on up to her crotch and practically nothing underneath, she might have been responsible. Not that we can censure Mrs. Adams too much for wearing so few clothes in all this heat."

Aunt Edie plain can't stand hot weather. Poor thing, she's tried every diet in the world but keeps getting bigger and bigger, and she really suffers in the summertime. Back when I was a little kid, she used to pay me twenty-five cents an hour to fan her with that big palmetto fan she carries around. I'd sit on the arm of her chair and try to look anywhere at all except down the front of her dress where the sweat poured down. And it *was* sweat. Mama can say until she's blue in the face that men sweat and ladies perspire, but my Aunt Edie sweats. She used to look up at me and wink. "What you looking for down in the valley?" she'd ask, and I couldn't help but giggle. I like Aunt Edie a lot. She's the oldest of Papa's sisters and practically the only one in the whole tribe of Casons and what's left of the Fairchilds—Mama's side of the family— who doesn't treat me like a baby.

Mrs. Dewberry was going into details about the way the murdered woman looked when they found her in the bathtub. "They say her eyes were almost popped out of her head because that nigger had tied the scarf around her neck so tight, and Dr. Waters said she had been raped, but, to tell the honest truth, I don't put much faith in anything that old fool Waters would say. And to be perfectly frank, I don't see how a body can tell if a married woman, especially a woman like Mrs. Adams, has been raped or not."

Aunt Edie let out a whoop of laughter. "I vow and declare, Sal Dewberry, you do say the most outrageous things."

"I wish you'd look who's talking! Well, it's true. That always did puzzle me when I read accounts in the paper, and believe me, the paper's chock-full of such things from front to back these days. It's bad enough to have them educated niggers and meddling Yankees stirring up trouble and freedom riding all over Alabama and Mississippi, without reading about rapes and murders and people setting fires all over the place. I've never seen anything to beat it in all my born days, and it makes me purely wonder what the world is coming to."

Mama murmured something, but Mrs. Dewberry drowned her out and kept on speaking and squeaking. "Of course, I hoped I'd be spared from seeing the day that such a thing would happen right here in Hines City. Every living soul in town is all worked up about it. I know because I had to make a trip in this morning to get some buttons. Naturally, Ernest said I didn't really need no buttons, that I had a Mack truck full now, and there wasn't no use to burn gas to go five miles to get buttons I didn't need. That husband of mine! He flat-out accused me of going in just to get all the news, but I noticed, however, that he went trucking along right with me. To get some nails, he said, but the whole blamed shed's full of nails. He talked with some of the men who joined up with Sheriff Wiggins last night. They took the bloodhounds and followed that boy's trail into the swamp, but lost it, God knows where. Believe me, I'm certainly planning to lock and bolt every window and door in my house tonight. And I don't intend to take a bath until they catch that low-down murderer."

Aunt Edie managed to get in a few words edgewise, which isn't easy when you're competing with Mrs. Dewberry. "Laura," she said to Mama, "if I were you, I wouldn't go worrying Tom with all this talk. He's had quite a bout with this terrible flu, and although he's getting better, praise the Lord, he still isn't well enough to get all excited. But you be extra careful about keeping things locked up here, too. I'm a mite worried about you and Sandy trying to manage alone with Tom still in his sickbed. I'm not trying to unduly alarm you, but the fact remains that nobody's got the dimmest notion where that boy's hiding, and I don't think you should take any chances until he's found and put behind bars."

Mama tried her best to reassure Aunt Edie. "Don't fret about me and Sandy. I doubt we've got a thing in the world to worry about, but I promise to lock the doors. That is, if I can locate a key. Heaven knows the last time these doors were locked—if ever. Now," she said brightly, "let's abandon this dismal topic and I'll go bring us out some refreshments. You two just sit and visit while I'm in the kitchen."

I could hear the screen door closing and the light swift tapping sound of Mama's feet going down the length of the hall.

"Well, Edie," Mrs. Dewsberry was saying in a somewhat lowered voice, "what do you want to bet she'll serve us as usual on the Fairchild silver tray with the very best crystal and china. It makes me all thumbs—scared to death I might break one of those precious tumblers. I think the world and all of Laura, but she sure does like to put on the dog."

"She's not putting on airs—it's just her way of doing things," said Aunt Edie. "I agree I'd be just as happy to drink my tea from a jelly glass, or Coke from a bottle, or whatever, but then, thank goodness, I'm not a Fairchild, which Laura is."

"A fact she's not about to let us forget. But I just hope for once she doesn't feel duty bound to tell us again about the Fairchild silver being hidden under a manure pile when Sherman was marching through."

"I agree, Sal. That story's a little threadbare. I'm confident I've heard it a dozen times."

And so had I. And at least a dozen times, on silver polishing days, I've wished with all my heart that General Sherman or his men had dug around in that pile of you-know-what and found every piece of it. Mama's got more than enough of everything to outfit a Morrison's Cafeteria.

Mrs. Dewberry was saying, "It's beyond me to fathom why Laura holds on to all those Fairchild ways. I'm even at a loss as to why she holds on to this drafty old Fairchild place. It's well over a hundred years old and constantly needing repairs, and it's far too big for just the four of them. Actually only the three of them, now that Benjie's in the navy. If I was her and Tom, I'd get shed of this mausoleum and put up one of those brand-new prefabs or even a double-wide mobile home—something snug and easy to manage. Laura doesn't seem to realize that we're living in the year of our Lord 1965 and the days of colored help is a thing of the past. All those cooks and washerwomen and cleaning girls we used to depend on are gone forever. I hear tell that some of the uppity rich

9

colored people have servants working for them, if you can imagine such a thing."

The tinkle of ice in glasses marked Mama's arrival on the porch. I could hear her apologizing. "You'll have to excuse this cake. I'm afraid it fell in the oven—it seems a little heavy."

That probably wasn't true—Mama's cakes never fall. They are always light and airy as clouds with heavenly icing. I could feel my mouth beginning to water, and then I sneezed. Not a little ladylike sneeze but a loud *kerchoo*. I almost scared those women out of seven years' growth. They yelped like stepped-on puppies, and all three faces rounded the corner.

Mama demanded in her give-me-no-nonsense voice, "Cassandra Cason, how long have you been sitting around the corner of that porch?"

"Not long, Mama. I thought you all knew I was there," I lied.

"How on earth could we know? It so happens that we don't have our eyes sticking out on stalks that bend a corner."

I tried to keep a straight face at the idea of that, and must have lucked out, since Mama sounded calmer when she continued. "You can march yourself right this minute and see if your father wants anything, and then you can go around back and feed those new turkey poults before dark."

Mrs. Dewberry had to put her two cents' worth in. "I do hope we haven't scandalized Sandy with our talk which wasn't meant for children. Little pitchers have big ears, you know."

All this little pitcher got from Aunt Edie was her usual grin and familiar wink as the three went back to their rockers.

CHAPTER 2

I walked around the house in pure disgust, wondering if the time would ever come when the grown-ups would include me instead of shooing me off. As a rule, I couldn't care less about their silly old talk, but today was different. Nobody's ever been murdered in Hines City that I know of, and for the sheriff and a posse to be out looking for a person I actually know, somebody from my school—that's enough to make anyone curious. And how could Mrs. Dewberry, with her big mouth, dare mention my big ears?

I stopped by Papa's window and pressed my nose against the screen. "Hey, Papa, it's me. Can I get you anything—a glass of water or something?"

"No, thank you, honey," he replied, and his voice sounded weak and trembly. I sure don't like for Papa to be sick like this. Papa is the glue that holds this family together, and things just aren't the same when he's laid up this way.

Papa's not a very big man when you measure him up against Aunt Edie and the rest of his sisters and brothers. They call him the runt of the Cason litter, and maybe he is, but he's awfully strong and sure of himself. He's got a serious side, but usually he's laughing and teasing and

11

full of jokes. Mama tries to calm him down, and she calls the Cason streak of foolishness downright common. "*Common* like in cold, or *common* like in everyday occurrences, or *common* like in poor white trash?" Papa will ask with his big Cason grin, and Mama only gets flustered.

Papa works for the government as a rural mail carrier, which is a pretty important job around these parts. His route covers the whole western section of Hines County. I bet all those folks will be glad when Papa gets well and back on the job. Old Mr. Groover, who substitutes, is slower than cold molasses and mixes everything up.

The turkeys and chickens are penned up next to the barn. It's not really a barn—more like a series of stalls and sheds all strung together at different heights. They used to hold all sorts of animals from goats to pigs to milk cows, and once, before Benjie left home to join the navy, a pet raccoon, which was certainly more trouble than it was worth. Everything's dilapidated and run down now, but I guess it doesn't matter, since Papa is not a farmer and never will be. When he and Mama first married, he turned some of the good land over and planted a small pecan grove, but that's the extent of his farming. He and Mama have a running battle about all those acres out there just going to waste. Papa would like to sell most of it off to the big Northern paper companies, but Mama can't bear to part with a grain of that Fairchild dirt. Sometimes she has to, of course, for taxes and hospital bills and major house repairs, but each time that happens she makes herself sick about it.

I sat down on an old cypress bench that used to hold washtubs back before drip-dry clothes and washing machines. Mama says when she was a little girl washday was one of her favorite days. She practically goes into raptures about blueing and Octagon soap and scrub boards, even rice water starch, and I pretend to be interested.

When Grandma and Grandpa Fairchild passed on right before Mama and Papa were married, this house was willed to Mama. Not only was the house handed down, but practically everything in it. Mama especially treasures the red leather family Bible on the living room table and the silver mint julep cups, the satin glass bowl, and the sterling napkin rings, which she keeps under lock and key in the china cabinet.

There was a time when the Fairchild family was very prominent here in south Georgia, back before the War Between the States, but I'm inclined to agree with Aunt Edie who declares that all we have left to show for it now is the prominent Fairchild nose. It skipped a generation when it bypassed Mama but I'm afraid I'm going to be stuck with it unless my face does a heap of growing. I used to feel like Jimmy Durante until Barbra Streisand came along. She's been a lot of comfort to me.

The sun was making me sleepy, so I forced myself to get up from the bench and feed those stupid turkeys. It was only the middle of the afternoon, and they didn't need feeding. Any half-wit could figure out that it was just an excuse for Mama to get rid of me.

I don't know why Mama even bothers raising turkeys. The frozen food section at the Winn Dixie supermarket has dozens of birds, ready for roasting, that I've never fed and watered and watched grow up. If we manage to get one raised up big enough for the table, it's like eating a member of the family.

When the turkeys were taken care of, I fastened the gate in the chicken-wire fence and struck out for the back of our property, determined not to set foot on the porch until Mama's company went home. I went through the edge of the worn-out orchard where the knotty little peaches had rotted without a chance to ripen. Scuffing my way through the fallen leaves, I reached the branch that trickles into the swamp about a quarter of a mile from our house. I love this swamp, even though it's not really good for anything. It's too wet to plow and too dry to fish, but it's a special place to me—full of secrets and magic. Even on the hottest day, it's always nice and cool.

It was quiet now, very still and quiet, and I thought of what I'd overheard and I felt a little flicker of fear. Glancing over my shoulder from time to time, I walked a little softer and tried not to make any noise, but that was even scarier. I finally decided I was acting downright silly, so I deliberately picked up a pine cone and hurled it up in a cedar tree, shattering the silence.

I was getting thirsty, so with noisy steps I walked on toward the big oak tree that holds my tree house. At the base of the tree is an old artesian well that's been flowing since slavery days. The cold clear water runs into an old horse trough made of a hollowed-out cypress. Benjie built the tree house a long time ago but he willed it to me when he joined the navy. Not that he had much choice, since he'd probably figured out I'd use it anyhow as soon as he was gone for good. Although he hadn't used it for years, he flatly refused to let me go near it while he was still home.

Benjie and I had never been real close. It wasn't just the difference in our ages—after all, Benjie is seventeen and I am still twelve. It was more than that. We were like two garments with the same Cason label, but cut from completely different bolts of cloth. But compared with some big brothers I guess he could have been worse. To my surprise, I miss him now that he's gone. When mention is made in the *Savannah Morning News* or on the Channel

12 TV station about places like Saigon or Da Nang, I always wonder is Benjie there. He never says much in the short, scrawled notes he occasionally sends.

I circled the edge of the branch on the way to the tree house and looked overhead at the trees. This swamp must have every kind of tree there is in the world. Besides the big live oaks, we've got magnolias, cypresses, fever trees—the fever tree is really a bay that gets its name because it blooms every year at the time folks around here used to get malaria—and there're also lots of cedars, pines, sweet gums and tupelos. I picked up a few of the tupelo berries and bit into one, which puckered my mouth. They're so all-fired sour, I poked the others in my pocket to eat back home, where I could put some salt on them.

It's so quiet inside the swamp, you can hear for miles, it seems. The gray moss drooping from the trees and the shiny bare cypress knees sticking up out of the water make it prettier than any church. There's one little spot where the branch widens out and makes a pool. A small speckled bream rippled the surface and I wished for my fishing pole. And I wished for Papa, who's my very favorite fishing buddy. Papa's been taking me fishing since I was knee-high to a duck, and I doubt there's a lake or a pond in the whole Altamaha swamp that we haven't fished in at one time or another.

The shadows were getting longer, so I lengthened my steps. If I planned to spend any time at all in my tree house, I had to hurry or the sun would start going down. Today, of all days, I wouldn't want dark to catch me this far away from home.

I reached the big oak and climbed up the rickety stairs that Benjie had nailed together. I tried to be careful because I tore my best pair of jeans on a loose nail not long

15

ago, and that almost put a stop to my trips to the tree house. Mama doesn't like for me to come here anyway. She feels it's not very ladylike, maybe not even safe, to wander around in the swamp, but there are times I've got to be by myself to figure things out. There couldn't be a better place just to sit and figure.

The second I reached the top of the tree and opened the door of the house I knew there was something wrong. It was real dim inside, and there wasn't a sound, but I sensed there was somebody in there. I stood there frozen while my eyes adjusted to the darkness. Then I blinked and saw him, plain as day. I had found Will Brown.

CHAPTER 3

I knew Will immediately although I'd only glimpsed him those few times with Benjie and watched him out on the football field, all covered up with heavy padding and a helmet. There wasn't any doubt in my mind as I stared at him, crouching in one corner, ready to spring. The whites of his eyes were gleaming and he had the longest, sharpest knife I ever saw in his hand.

I don't know how long we stood there staring at each other—not speaking, scarcely breathing. I tried to ease myself back out the door.

"Oh no, you don't," Will growled in a real tough voice. "Don't you make a move and don't you make a noise. Don't you even lift a hand, or I'll—" The threat trailed away but he kept on holding that wicked-looking knife in the air. Then he made a beckoning motion. "Come over here and have a seat, real easy like, while I do some thinking."

I stumbled toward an empty orange crate and sat on the edge, and Will stood up a little straighter and was towering over me. That tree house isn't very big, and we were so close together we were breathing on each other—ragged, uneven breaths—and that was the only sound in the room.

I finally summoned up the courage to speak. "Now you listen here, my name is Sandy Cason and this is my property, and I want to know what the heck you're doing up here." Although my voice came out in a squeak even worse than Mrs. Dewberry's, I still sounded braver than I felt.

I thought at first he wasn't going to answer, but then he mumbled something I couldn't quite catch. I waited and he repeated, "My name is Will. Will Brown." He stopped, as though that said it all. I kept on waiting. I also watched with relief as he folded that awful knife and slid it into his pocket.

Will repeated my name, "Cason. Are you any kin to Benjie Cason?" He answered his own question. "Yeah, you'd have to be, I reckon, since this is Cason land."

"He's my brother. But he isn't here and you are, and I want to know why." I was still scared but felt a little bolder with that knife tucked out of sight and the clenched look easing up a little on Will's face. "You still haven't told me what you're doing up here." I knew most of it, of course, but I needed Will to put it in words. Maybe then it would quit seeming like some terrible dream.

"Why am I here? I'll be darned if I know," Will said. Then, as though he had to talk to somebody or bust, words started pouring out. "What's today—Saturday? Well, it all started yesterday. I'd been down cleaning yards for a woman named Mrs. Adams—maybe this far out of town you didn't know her—you probably wouldn't know her anyway—and when I finished raking I went on home. And I hadn't been there mor'n thirty or forty minutes when Uncle Pete—that's my uncle who preaches at the African Baptist Church—came flying in to tell me there was a lot of commotion downtown. It seems

18

somebody had choked Mrs. Adams to death. There was some people—especially her husband, who'd gotten back to town and found her body in the bathtub—saying I'd done it." He jabbed at his chest with his middle fingers, making a thumping sound. "Me, Will Brown! Can you believe they'd think I did it?" His hands dropped by his side, palms up, and he shook his head.

For the life of me, I didn't know what to say. But Will went on, talking more to himself than to me. "That's when I lost my head and acted like a plain old fool and started running. I didn't stop to think. All I wanted to do was get away—but fast—until somebody straightened out the mess. Until they found out who did it, 'cause it sure as heck wasn't me."

Will folded his arms across his chest and propped himself against the wall, resting most of his weight on his right leg. He looked and sounded exhausted. "I headed out through the woods and I kept on running and running till I got to the swamp and I kept moving all night. By that time I was calling myself every name in the book for taking off like that, but now I had no choice but to keep going. I got into the water in this branch right about where your Pa's land joins old Mr. Tatum's land. I figured maybe if I waded in the water they wouldn't find my tracks and the hounds couldn't follow me." Will swallowed and took a deep breath. "Well, I just kept going and going and could've kept right on except I fell, jumping over a ditch, and hurt my ankle. The left one here," he said, pointing. "Either sprained or broke it, and took most of the skin right off my leg. I plain couldn't make it no further after that."

"How did you manage to find my tree house?" I asked.

"Just lucky, I guess. Even though it's tucked way back here in the woods and pretty well hidden, I remembered

Benjie pointing it out a long time ago on one of our hunting trips. Besides, it was cracking daylight by the time I reached here, so I dragged myself up to rest. I thought I might be able to hide in here until my leg gets better. It's all swollen up and I can't move on it now." Having said all this, he gave me a long, hard look—a measuring look—and suddenly I was scared all over again. "I guess those plans just bombed. I hadn't counted on you showing up."

His tone of voice put me on the defensive. "I've got every right to come down here. After all, it's my tree house now that Benjie's in the navy."

Will didn't say a word. He just kept sizing me up with those steady eyes.

I tried again. "Well, since I did show up, what are you planning to do?"

Will shrugged. "I'm fresh out of plans. You got any suggestions?"

"None that make sense," I admitted. "But you can't stay here, that's for sure."

"You're right about that. This is much too close to Hines City for comfort." He shook his head impatiently. "If only I hadn't hurt my leg, I'd be long gone by now." He took a few experimental steps. The pain made him squinch his eyes, and little beads of sweat popped out on his face.

Alarmed, I cried out, "Hey, cut it out—and, for goodness' sake, sit down before you fall down." I reached out but didn't quite touch him.

Will slumped to the floor, easing his legs out in front of him, and mopped at his brow with the back of his hand. He looked dreadful, and I just knew for sure he was going to faint. His face was the color of gray river mud, and his eyes were wide and glassy.

I'm not all that good in emergencies, but I had to do something. Whirling around, I backed down the wobbly stairs and ran to the well where I filled an old hollow drinking gourd full of water. Without spilling too much of it, I managed to climb back up into the tree house and thrust it in Will's hand. "Here, drink this," I commanded.

"OK, Sergeant," Will said, with a faint trace of a smile.

Relieved, I watched his face return to a color approaching normal. "Well, that settles that," I said at last.

"Settles what?"

"It's plain as day you aren't going anywhere—at least not now. You've got to stay put until your leg gets better."

"Sure seems that way," said Will in a hopeless voice.

"What are you going to do?"

"I wish you'd quit asking me that," he snapped. "I've told you I haven't got any answers."

"What about your family?" I suggested. "Isn't there somebody I could phone to come pick you up?"

"No," Will said vehemently, getting that hard, cold look again, "don't you dare do that." Then, a little calmer, he added, "Besides, there isn't anybody but Uncle Pete, and the law is probably watching every move he makes. I'd bet my bottom dollar they've tapped his phone."

Suddenly, right or wrong, I made a decision. "Will, this might not be the safest place on earth, but you can stay on here if you want to while you're waiting for your leg to heal."

"Yeah, sure—and have you run back home and blabber it all over the countryside. No thank you."

"But I wouldn't. Honest, I wouldn't tell a soul."

"Except your mamma and daddy and a dozen of your friends."

"Go ahead, be sarcastic, but I really wouldn't tell. Papa's sick so I wouldn't tell him, and I tell Mama precious little I don't have to. And I don't have a dozen friends. As a matter of fact," I added, "I have practically no friends outside of Wanda Dewberry, and we're not speaking." That wasn't exactly true, but close enough for the moment.

Will looked at his injured leg for a long moment, then lifted his head and looked me straight in the eye. "I guess I've got no choice but to trust you. But I'm telling you right now, if you turn me in, I'll come back and haunt you till your dying day." He ran both hands through his hair. "I never did actually hear them, but I know as good as I know my name that the sheriff's got his bloodhounds out and rounded up a posse, and they'll keep on beating the bushes until they catch me. And once they find me, I'll have no chance to tell them I didn't kill that woman. As God is my witness, I never laid a hand on her. That's the honest truth."

I shuddered. This was no longer like a dream but an out-and-out nightmare. I managed to say, "I believe you, Will. I'm sure you didn't hurt that woman." I couldn't bring myself to say the word *murder* out loud.

Will gave a short little laugh. "Besides knocking a few heads around on the football field, I don't recall ever hurting a living soul. That's why this whole thing's so stupid. Before yesterday I'd never even had a speeding ticket, and here I am now on the verge of being lynched."

"Don't say that," I begged. "But you're right about the posse. The sheriff and his men are looking for you all over the place. When your leg gets better, where are you planning to run to?"

"As soon as I can, I'll try to get across the border into Florida. I got a brother, Big Bubba, who works on a shrimp boat out of Mayport. He can get me a job down there. He tried his best to talk me down there last year, to finish up school and work part time, and I should have gone. Then I wouldn't be in this mess." Will slapped his fist into the palm of his other hand. "I also should've listened when he told me to stay away from that woman —that she wasn't nothing but trouble."

"Did your brother know her?"

"Not really. Like everybody else in town, he knew about her. But he was right—from the very beginning, that woman was real bad news. Like Uncle Pete says, she was brazen as a daughter of Satan." He looked over at me. "Hey, you probably go into Hines City to school, and you might know my Uncle Pete. During the week, when he's not preaching, he's the janitor at the school."

Will sounded so eager for me to know his uncle that I hated to admit that I didn't. Although I dimly remembered a coveralled figure cleaning up the school grounds, I'd never really looked at him or paid him any attention.

I glanced outside and could tell by the sun that it was going on six o'clock and almost time for supper. The thought occurred that Will probably hadn't had a bite to eat since he started running. He must be starving to death. All I had in my pocket were some boiled peanuts and those danged old tupelo berries, and goodness knows not even a starving man can do much with those sour things. Silently I handed over the peanuts and Will gulped them down in a couple of bites.

"Will, I'll tell you what I'll do. If I possibly can, I'll sneak you a bite down here after supper." Will's face brightened and I held up my hand. "Now don't go counting on it, please, because with all this excitment, Mama's liable not to let me out of her sight. You know how peculiar mothers can be."

"It would be even more peculiar if she wasn't concerned," said Will, sounding very grown-up. "After all, there's a murderer on the loose somewhere out there, and it might pay to be careful."

I knew I was gawking at Will, but I couldn't help it. It had suddenly dawned on me that in all my life I'd never said more than two or three words to a black boy. The only one in our class keeps pretty much to himself and might as well have lockjaw for all the talking he does. Now here I was, not only talking to a black boy, but listening to him lecture me like a brother or something. The whole thing seemed unreal. I felt unreal, standing there like Lot's wife, or whoever it was that turned into a pillar of salt.

Will crinkled his eyes and smiled, trying to get through to me. "What's the matter, Sandy? Is my face on crooked or something?"

I tried to smile back, but all I could manage was a wave good-bye as I backed down the stairs. I had to get home before Mama came looking for me. That would be sheer disaster, for just as sure as she caught wind of the fact that Will was hiding out on our land, she'd feel it was her Christian duty to tell Sheriff Wiggins. And sure as shooting, she'd tell Papa, sick or not, and I plain don't know what he would do. We don't really talk about it, but I know that Papa's got a thing about blacks. He says they're fine as long as they know their place and stay in it, but I'm willing to bet that never in a zillion years would he consider my tree house a proper place for a black boy.

Mama's company had left, thank goodness, and supper was on the kitchen table. I looked around the room. From the African violets on the windowsill to the braided rug on the floor, everything looked the way it always looked, and yet it was somehow different. I couldn't shake off the feeling that I was caught up in the middle of a dream that threw everything out of focus. It was all I could do to sit still while Mama asked the blessing.

Mama seemed busy with her own private thoughts, so we didn't talk much while we ate. I had one bad moment when she said, "Well, Sandy, since you didn't bother to announce your presence on the porch this afternoon, I'm sure you drank in all the details of yesterday's murder."

Apparently she didn't expect an answer, for after a pause she continued, "I wonder if they've caught that poor colored boy."

I had to say something to keep her from seeing how fidgety I was. "Mama, why do you keep saying *colored*? They prefer to be called *blacks*."

Mama tossed her head. "That's ridiculous, Sandy. I was raised to say *colored people* to show respect. Colored folks would have been highly indignant—and rightly so—if we had called them *black*."

It doesn't pay to argue with Mama. It's like trying to push a car up a hill with a rope.

Supper seemed to stretch on for ages, and I kept sneaking glances at the kitchen clock. This time of year it doesn't get good and dark until almost eight o'clock, but even so I had little more than an hour to get some food to Will. I calculated my best bet would be to try and do it while Mama was feeding Papa. She takes his meals on a tray and sits with him while he eats, and then they usually talk for a little while.

I looked at Mama, who was slowly, deliberately, cutting a slice of pork into bite-sized pieces. I thought it's no wonder people keep saying that Mama was the prettiest girl ever to grow up in Hines County. She's small—not much larger than me—and her hair is the color of wild clover honey. Her eyes are as blue as a robin's eggs. If this makes Mama sound like a china doll, you can take my word she isn't. There are times she's as soft as a marshmallow and I can talk her into anything I want, but most of the time she's as hard as the shell on a black walnut, and she can't be budged. Mama loves me, I know, but she's not much for hugging and kissing. When I feel the need to be petted, it's Papa I turn to.

Finally supper was over, and Mama got up, fixed Papa's tray, and left the kitchen. I didn't waste another minute. Grabbing up three biscuits, an ear of boiled corn, a large piece of pork, and a red tomato from the window-sill, I crammed them into an empty paper bag from the pantry. Listening hard, I could hear low voices from Mama and Papa's bedroom as I eased open the back screen door.

The sky was streaked with a misty violet color in the early twilight as I made my way down the weed-choked path. When I reached the foot of the oak tree, I gave a low, soft whistle but I didn't get an answer. I realized why. From what I'd heard at school, Will was practically a genius—not many guys can captain a football team and still make the honor roll—so he certainly had more sense than to answer just any old whistle.

I climbed up and called his name as I pushed the slat-ted door inward. Will stood near the opening, tilted a little, favoring his bad leg. Again he had that shiny knife in his hand, half raised in the air in a threatening way.

"It's only me," I said hurriedly, holding out the sack. His face relaxed a little and he pocketed the knife. Sniff-ing the food I'd brought him, he said, "Smells good. My stomach was beginning to think my throat's been cut."

It wasn't a very good joke but at least he was trying.

26

"Go on and eat while it's halfway warm," I urged. "I hurried as fast as I could."

Will said between bites, "I've been sitting here wondering if you'd make it back at all."

"I promised I would."

"You promised to try." He took another swallow.

I looked hard at Will, sitting there on the floor with the paper bag open between his knees. In the half-light of the little room, he didn't look nearly as big as he had earlier today. It was almost as though his hurting leg and exhaustion had shrunken him up. And besides, no matter how tough he tried to act, I could tell deep down he was scared. "Look, Will, try not to worry too much. Maybe things will be better in the morning when I come to check on you."

"Sure," he said with a weary sigh. "By the way, next time why don't you whistle like this"—and he gave two shorts and a long, not raising his voice above the whispering level we'd been using—"and then I'll know it's you."

I practiced just as softly and Will said, "Well, all right— that's pretty good for a girl."

Ignoring that remark, I moved toward the opening and then turned back. "Good night."

Will missed a couple of beats before replying, "Good night, Sandy Cason." His face was solemn and he had that measuring look again, obviously wondering whether or not he could really trust me.

I was barely out of sight of the tree house before *my* doubts set in. I was taking an awful chance! How could I know for sure that I could trust Will Brown? He might look harmless and sound innocent, but how could I know for sure? Papa's always said that no white person could trust a black to show his true feeling—that there isn't any

27

way to tell what a black is thinking. He says from the time they're born, they only let us white folks see what they want us to see, especially here in the South.

I've always gone along with what Papa says, because I don't know much about blacks. I'd only bumped into a handful before the schools and the buses and the restaurants were integrated, which didn't take place in Hines County until a couple of years ago. I've tried to make friends with the few in my class—especially Lilly Mae Crandall and Sadie Cooper, who live next door to each other in a little black settlement two or three miles down the road—but nothing much has come of it. I've never been invited to their houses and they've never been to mine. It's hard to be friends with all that distance between us.

Now here I am all of a sudden ignoring Papa's opinions and taking a mighty big step on my own, not even stopping to think the whole thing through. For all I know, I might be getting mixed up in something that could pull me in over my head and get me in a whole heap of trouble. I suddenly wanted to rush right home and dump the whole problem in my parents' lap and let them deal with it, but I simply couldn't. Common sense told me that Will was no more a murderer than I was, and besides, I'd given him my word that I wouldn't rat on him. A promise is a promise.

CHAPTER 4

With my heart thudding heavy against my ribs, I ran back home through the gathering dusk. I went around to the front porch and sank down in the swing, mopping the perspiration from my forehead with my shirt sleeve and trying to slow my breathing before I encountered Mama.

My breath was still coming out like an asthma attack when Sheriff Wiggins and three of his men pulled into our driveway. Parking his brand-new '65 Buick dangerously close to one of Mama's prize camellias, the sheriff got out and started swaggering up to the porch. He left his men in the car, but my mouth went completely dry when I saw that he had two of his smelly old bloodhounds with him on a chain, and it was all I could do to reply when he asked if Mama was home. I managed to mumble a couple of words when Mama, who must have heard the sheriff drive up, stepped out on the porch.

"Mrs. Cason," the sheriff said without even taking off his hat, "I sure do hate to bother you all with Tom sick the way he is, but I was just wonderin' if you'd seen or heard anythin' out of the ordinary. We're lookin' for that murderin' bast— Excuse me, I mean heathen—who killed that poor defenseless Miz Adams in her bathtub."

"I assure you, Sheriff, we haven't noticed a thing. Do you have any reason to believe he's out this way?"

The sheriff shifted the wad of chewing tobacco around in his jaw with a squishy sound that made me shudder. "No'm, not really, ma'am. That bone-headed posse of mine let him get away last night, and there ain't no tellin' where that nigger's hidin' out."

Mama stiffened at the word *nigger*. That's one word she hates to hear in this house, although she's never figured out a way to keep the Dewberrys from using it. Her voice was cool and very ladylike. "Sheriff Wiggins, if we hear or see anything, I'll call you immediately."

"Much obliged to you, ma'am." The sheriff turned to leave. "I'll be biddin' you good evenin' now, but you be sure to give old Tom my best regards."

The sheriff moved closer in my direction and leaned over the edge of the porch to spit his tobacco juice. Until now his bloodhounds had stayed fairly still and quiet, but suddenly they were straining at their leash and sniffing the legs of my blue jeans. I wondered if they could smell Will on me. I sat there, holding my breath. Even so, the sheriff noticed the bloodhounds acting peculiar. Giving them a little more rein, he eyed the dogs as they moved closer and closer, panting and slobbering over my knees, which were all but knocking together.

"Well, little lady," he said—and if there's anything I hate to be called, it's *little lady*, especially by people I can't stand—"I know it's flat-out impossible, but the way my dawgs are actin' makes me wonder if you know more'n you're tellin'."

"Really, Sheriff Wiggins," Mama said, drawing herself up to her fullest height, "what on earth are you suggesting?"

The sheriff gave her a sheepish grin. "Nothin' a-tall ma'am. But you must admit these dawgs are showin' a powerful lot of interest in your daughter. Can't figger out what's gotten into them."

"Well, neither can I," Mama said haughtily. "Perhaps they merely want to leave."

Even the sheriff could take a hint that broad. He said good-bye again and clomped down the steps, yanking the hounds behind him. After he was gone, Mama turned to me. "For the life of me, I can't imagine what that was all about."

I didn't say anything. I just sat there, glad that it was almost pitch-dark now so my face couldn't give me away.

Mama looked hard in my direction. "Sandy, you might not like Sheriff Wiggins—for that matter, neither do I— but you really ought to show more respect for your elders. You were barely civil to him." She paused for a long moment. "Come to think of it, you're behaving rather strange anyway. I think perhaps you need a good purging—you might be coming down with the flu like your father."

My stomach did flip-flops. It would really test me if I had to choose between helping Will and taking a dose of castor oil and epsom salts, which is what Mama gives as a purgative. I sat small in the swing and Mama turned and went back into the house.

The longer I lay in bed that night, the wider awake I got. I couldn't quit thinking about Will out there in the tree house. I could hear some hoot owls way back in the swamp, and I could imagine how lonely and scared he must be. I know about being lonely since most of the time, when I'm not in school, there's nobody but me to

31

keep me company. Of course, occasionally, there's Papa when he's not working, and, once in a while, there's Mama. But Mama's been so sad and worried since Benjie dropped out of school and went off to Vietnam that she's like a different person. I can hardly remember the last time we went blackberry picking, or walked in the woods, or went visiting, or just sat and talked together. It seems to me that Mama's not interested in much of anything now except the war news and what she calls the good old days that are past and over with. She still finds time and energy to go to the monthly meetings of the DAR. That stands for the Daughters of the American Revolution, but Papa's definition is funnier: Dull And Ridiculous. Mama explodes every time Papa pokes fun at the work she's doing on her family genealogy. She's deadly serious about it. It's like a religion to her.

From way off in the distance came the baying of a hound—a mournful, chilling sound. Most likely it was one of old Mr. Tatum's pack, but I couldn't be sure. I tried to tell myself that Will was perfectly safe. That even if the posse found him, they'd believe his story. But I knew better. A man like Sheriff Wiggins would do something awful to Will and not ask questions until later.

Eventually I went to sleep, but I bet I woke up a dozen times. It must have been almost daylight when the rain began, but it was still too dark to see the round face of the alarm clock ticking away on the bureau. Usually I like to listen to the rain. The drumming sound on the roof overhead makes a warm cave of my covers, and the small limbs of the chinaberry tree brushing against the windowpanes are friendly fingers. But this morning I found myself sitting bolt upright in the middle of the bed. That tree house was probably leaking like a wornout sieve, and I could almost see Will huddled in a corner, drenched to the skin. Things were bad enough without him getting double pneumonia, and there wasn't a darned thing I could do at this point to help him. I just kept on sitting in the bed, and to use one of Benjie's expressions, feeling as useless as teats on a boar.

The rain finally stopped and I got up with the sun, which is a fairly dumb thing to do on a Sunday morning. I put on yesterday's jeans but a fresh tee shirt and picked up a brush and stared at myself in the mirror. I've never been much to look at, but now I really look like a scarecrow. Mama has always maintained I'd look a little more human if I'd let my hair grow out to a decent length, but I can't convince myself I'm the rollers and bobby pins type. Lord knows I have no choice now but to let it grow out some, since it isn't more than two or three inches long any place on my head, thanks to Wanda Dewberry. Wanda's whole ambition is to be a beauty operator and, like a fool, I let her get hold of me about a month ago.

In my opinion, my hair was awful enough to begin with—half-and-half red and brown with a cowlick sticking straight up—but it wasn't one of my major problems. It became one in a hurry when Wanda got through butchering and vanished back to the Dewberry house. Mama was tempted to choke me with the apron she draped around my sholders when she tried to even it up. Through clenched teeth, she hissed, "If you ever"—*snip* —"let Wanda Dewberry"—*snip*—"get near you with a pair of scissors again"—*snip, snip*—"I vow I'll disown you—and report her to the juvenile court." I don't think she meant it, but with Mama I can never be sure; so to play it safe, I swore I'd let Wanda practice on somebody else in the future.

Papa was sitting in the corner of the kitchen during Mama's barbering, and even he had laughed at me—not *with* me but *at* me—and that was punishment enough. I guess he couldn't help it—I did look pretty gross.

Mama waved the shears again and snipped at a few more tufts. "It's bad enough for you to act like a tomboy—you don't have to dress the part." She was almost in tears. "There are times I have trouble believing you're my natural daughter, my very own flesh and blood."

"That's enough, Laura," Papa said in an easy voice, but it silenced Mama. Winking at me, he added, "Besides, Sandy's not a tomboy. You're a Tom-girl, aren't you, honey?" That's one of our private jokes, since his name is Tom and I'm his girl.

Giving my cowlick one last swipe, I wedged my hairbrush in between an autographed picture of the Beatles and a blurry snapshot of Benjie in his navy uniform. Next to that was a baby photograph of Wanda and me together in my playpen, peering out at the world like two monkeys in a cage. Wanda and I have known each other all our lives, and we used to be best friends, but things are different now. One of us must be changing, and I think it's her. We still see a lot of each other, of course, and talk back and forth on the phone, but something is missing. We don't giggle and carry on like we used to, and those secrets we used to share no longer seem all that important. Even though she won't come right out and admit it, she's traded me in for boys. I just hope she doesn't turn into a sex maniac like her sister Pearl.

I decided all of a sudden that I'd make a flying trip to the swamp and check on Will before the day got started, but Mama stopped me in the kitchen. Several slices of cured ham were curling their edges in the skillet. Fork in hand, Mama turned from the stove, "Morning, Sandy. How does grits and red eye gravy sound to you?"

"Fine, Mama." I had no choice but to settle myself at

the kitchen table. "How's Papa?" I asked, looking for any safe topic.

"He had a fairly good night. I think he's over the worst of it." She sighed and pushed a strand of hair away from her face. "It's really a shame he has to miss church today. He looks forward all year to Homecoming Day and dinner on the ground. I guess you'll have to represent the Cason family."

"Oh, Mama," I practically wailed, "could I please stay home today? I've got too much to do to go to church."

Mama's eyes lifted. "Like what?"

"Like homework and memorizing the Gettysburg Address for Commencement and—"

Mama cut me short. "You'll have all afternoon and evening to do that in. As far as that goes, you could do it now before church. You've still got hours." She cracked the oven door to check on the biscuits. "However, I've arranged with the Dewberrys to pick you up, so make sure you're ready in plenty of time."

Finally, Mama put my breakfast before me, saying without any note of apology in her voice, "Sorry, Sandy —these are real racehorse grits this morning." It was one of Mama's typical jokes. I think it meant that the grits were so thin and runny it would take a racehorse to catch them, but I hesitated to ask. The best thing to do with Mama's jokes is leave them alone.

From her place at the table across from me, Mama looked out the kitchen window. "I am *so* glad the sun is shining. It's a perfect day for the church dinner. Not only that, I kept fretting about that poor colored boy in that pouring-down rain."

I could feel myself sinking lower in my chair as Mama kept on talking. "I still think the whole idea of that boy committing a murder is downright absurd. There might have been times when Benjie seemed lacking in good judgment but I'm convinced he wouldn't have associated himself with anyone capable of such an act." She stopped to butter a biscuit. "I admit, I never could really see why Benjie spent so much time with Will, but he seemed nice enough, even if he was colored. And he certainly came from a good family. The Browns have always been known as quality colored people, not like some of the no-account uppity kind that are getting so unbearable lately." She interrupted herself to admonish, "Straighten your shoulders, Cassandra—you're all slouched over," and then continued, "I purely hate to go into Hines City lately with some of the colored folks getting so pushy and grabby. There are times I long for the old days when people tried harder to get along with each other. Things are so different now." She paused to stir her coffee, and I silently wished for a pot to boil over or Papa to call or something, anything, that would shut Mama up and let me get out of there. "Yes, Sandy, back in the old days you could actually love a person no matter what race he belonged to. I guess you remember how much I loved Aunt Polly." Her voice threatened to break and she stopped talking.

"I remember, Mama." And I did. Mama had truly loved her old black nurse, Aunt Polly. And when Aunt Polly died a year ago, Mama had cried her heart out at the funeral. She still grieves when she thinks about her, but I'm stuck with the notion that Mama's love for Aunt Polly had nothing to do with color. Aunt Polly was the last living, breathing thing from Mama's past, and that's why Mama felt so sad when she had to let her go.

Mama got up from the table and started preparing Papa's tray, saying over her shoulder, "Well, there's one thing about it—I'm certainly much more tolerant than your father. He'll tell you right off that he's got no use for the way the government is cramming this integration down our throats. He feels we're being pressured, and perhaps he's right."

Papa would be foaming at the mouth, I thought miserably, if he knew about Will. Papa's the smartest and fairest man in the world about most things, and I've always felt free to go to him with my problems. But now, with the biggest problem of my whole life, I couldn't depend on him to help me. I was strictly on my own.

As soon as Mama disappeared into the bedroom with Papa's breakfast tray, I grabbed up the leftover ham and a couple of biscuits and a whole jar of fig preserves from a pantry shelf. Then I ran to the linen closet in the hall and snatched up a sheet and a couple of towels and ducked out the back kitchen door.

Outside, in the plunder room, which holds odds and ends of practically everything, I found an empty croaker sack, a half-used bar of Octagon soap, an old tarpaulin, a hammer, and a pocketful of nails. I stuffed everything, including the food, in the burlap sack until it looked like a loosely packed beanbag. Slinging it over my shoulder, I raced in the direction of the swamp, my head half-turned, expecting with every step to hear Mama call but having no earthly idea what to say if she did. I let out my breath with a *whoosh* when I reached the orchard and stopped to rest, laying the heavy sack in the path at my feet.

Off in the distance were the ruins of a few little cabins that were quarters for the Fairchild slaves back in plantation days. Now there's nothing much left but cypress pillars and posts, and a few scattered handmade bricks grown over with blackberry vines. Mama used to walk with me and point out where the stables once held the riding horses, where the curing sheds and tobacco barns once stood, the smoke house, the pigeon cotes, the syrup boilers—all the things that made this a working farm. Most of these things were already gone when Mama was a little girl and walked with her mother, who pointed out the way things used to be in the old days. But Mama acts like it's all still standing.

A covey of quail made a whirring sound as they rose into the air from the nearest patch of weeds. I had rested enough, so I gathered up the croaker sack, slung it over my shoulder again, and went on my way.

When I reached the base of the tree house, I tried the signal we'd agreed on the evening before. It worked, for almost at once, Will poked his head out of the little door. I climbed up slowly, dragging the heavy sack behind me. Will reached out and helped me up the last two steps, neither of us saying a word, not even good morning.

Silently Will watched as I dumped the things in the middle of the floor. "Here," I said at last, retrieving the food from the middle of the pile and handing it to him, "here's your breakfast. You must be starving."

Will took the burlap sack and sat down on the floor, with his bad leg sticking straight out. "Thanks," he said, and took out a biscuit.

Sounding like a moron, I asked, "Did it rain out here?"

"Cats and dogs. I thought for sure I was gonna go down for the third and last time," Will said glumly.

"I know. I thought about you, 'cause Benjie was behind the door when the Lord was passing out carpenter skills. I hope for the sake of this whole country, they don't want him to do any building in the navy." I looked up where the sun was beaming through the cracks. "How bad did it leak?"

"Well, at first it was pretty bad—more like it was rain-ing in here and leaking outside. But I scrooched over in that far corner where the roof was more in one piece and almost found a dry spot."

I remembered the tarp. Will, laying his breakfast aside and hobbling around on one foot, helped me spread it against the slatted roof and, together, we managed to nail it to the boards. It wasn't the neatest job I ever saw, but it would serve the purpose. Then, without explaining, I climbed back down the ladder and gathered up the driest of the fallen moss from the ground and carried it back up, three or four loads in all, and patted it into a bed shape in the likeliest looking corner. I pulled out the largest sticks and twigs and threw them out of either what Benjie had designed as a window or else was just a larger crack than the others.

When, finally, I had done the best I could, I spread the clean sheet over it and it looked like a fairly decent bed. Will and I sat on the floor and stared at it in silence. "Well," I said with a sigh, "I guess it's better than no bed at all."

"It's fine, Sandy. I appreciate your lugging all that stuff up here. Besides," he added, "I hope I won't be needing it more than a night or so. I've got to get gone from here. If only"—and with this he struck his thigh with a balled-up fist—"I hadn't hurt this doggone leg."

Screwing up all my courage, I said, "Pull up your jeans and let me take a look at that leg."

"I can do better than that." Will reached in his pocket for his knife, and the tree house was filled with the raspy sound of the blade making long, jagged cuts as he whacked his blue jeans off at the knee.

I looked, and immediately wished I hadn't. Will's leg was terribly swollen and scratched, and there were puffy, dark red streaks snaking up his calf. My ham and grits made a knot in my stomach, and I swallowed hard before I said, "Gee, Will, it's coming along fine, seems to me."

Will smiled a crooked half-smile and shook his head. "Sandy, you make out pretty good as one of those Samaritans they told us about in Sunday School, but you're no great shakes at lying."

"And I'm no great shakes at doctoring, either," I mumbled. "We've got to get you some help." I wished I could tell Mama about Will—she'd know what to do.

"No, you can't do that," Will said harshly. Then his voice softened a little. "Don't worry about the leg. I'll just keep rubbing it with the turpentine you brought and it's bound to get better." Trying to sound convincing, he added, "It feels to me like the swelling is going down, and it honestly doesn't pain me as much as it did."

I let that pass. Instead, I said, "Will, I guess I ought to tell you—when I got home last evening, Sheriff Wiggins and some of his men stopped by."

"And?"

"And you're right. You've got to get away as soon as you can. That posse's out there looking all over for you."

Will's hand shot out and clamped my arm like a vise, scaring me a little. "Tell me," he demanded, "do you know where they're looking?"

"No—no," I stammered. "The sheriff didn't say."

"Sorry," Will said, releasing my arm. After a moment he added in a low, discouraged voice, "It really doesn't matter where they're looking right now—sooner or later they'll stumble on this part of the swamp."

I tried to reassure him. "Maybe not, Will. That dumb old Sheriff Wiggins doesn't have the sense that God gave a billy goat. He probably couldn't find his own shadow." I glanced at Will whose jaw was still set, and his eyes were despairing. "I hate that man—I mortally despise him."

Will's face was relaxing a little. "That's pretty strong, Sandy. What did the sheriff ever do to you?"

"Nothing personal," I admitted, "but that's not the point. He's always popping up out of nowhere pretending to be a friend of my father's, but Papa can't stand him either. Not only that, he used to pay us calls about Benjie—friendly warnings, he'd say, about speed laws and drag racing and littering the highway with beer bottles— nothing major. But he'd scare the living daylights out of me every time he showed up, him and his old cruiser with the red light blinking."

Getting to my feet, I stood by the door. "I gotta go before Mama misses me—which she's probably done already. She's probably out looking for me this very minute."

Will's smile vanished completely, and I hastily added, "Don't worry about it—Mama won't come this far. She just stands in the peach orchard and yells in every direction. She knows I won't go beyond the sound of her voice without telling her first."

Will folded his arms across his chest and looked across at me. "Speaking of telling, are you sure you haven't said anything to anybody about me being here?"

"Not a word to a soul," I said, fingering the front of my shirt, "cross my heart, hope to die." Now it was my turn to look at Will. "What's the matter? Don't you trust me?"

Will gave a little shrug but didn't say anything.

"Well, do you or don't you?" I asked, feeling both hurt and angry. Here I was risking my neck, and he wouldn't even talk to me.

"Sure, I trust you, Sandy—it's just that I've been

thinking. You're just a kid—and a girl—and this whole thing could turn out to be a very nasty business. Maybe you shouldn't get involved."

I thought for a moment. "Looks to me like I'm already involved. You're here and I know you're here, so I can't just snap my fingers and forget it, now can I?"

"No," Will said slowly, "I guess you can't. But you be extra careful. I don't want you getting hurt."

"Oh pooh," I said lightly, "nothing's gonna happen to me, except Mama might pinch my head off if I don't go dress for church. It's Homecoming Day with dinner on the ground, and, since she can't leave Papa, I've got to represent the whole Cason family."

"While you're gone, I'll stretch out here on my new bed and think about all that food. If it's anything like our church, you'll have enough food to feed Pharaoh's army. Eat enough for both of us, you hear?"

"Sure, Will," I promised.

CHAPTER 5

Mama was in the kitchen packing a wicker basket with food. *"Deviled* eggs and *angel* food cake might make strange bedfellows, Sandy, but if you handle them gently, I think you can make it to the church without any ruckus." That was a better than average joke for Mama.

As I turned to leave, she asked me point-blank, "Where have you been for the last hour?"

"Nowhere, Mama, really."

She looked me straight in the eye. "There are times I find your behavior truly baffling. When I want peace and quiet, it seems you're underfoot asking a million questions, but the next thing I know you're gone like a streak of greased lightning and I can't find you anywhere. Sandy, where were you?"

"I told you, Mama—nowhere," I answered, as I escaped from the kitchen.

I hurriedly dressed for church and went, with sash dangling, to see Papa. He was propped up in bed, drinking coffee from his favorite mug, while Mama flicked imaginary dust from the bureau.

"Are you still contagious, Papa?"

"Mama says not," he replied with a grin. "She's even

quit poking pills at me every time I turn around. Come give me an overdue kiss."

Leaning over, I kissed his freshly shaved cheek, loving the Old Spice smell. When I straightened up, he looked me over. "My, but don't we look pretty this morning?"

"Pretty is as pretty does," said Mama, tackling the sash. "But at least you're taking your pocketbook this morning. I haven't seen it since Easter." She sighed. "It's really a waste to buy nice things for you."

Suddenly the pocketbook hooked over my left arm seemed as big as a laundry hamper. Mama was right, of course—I hadn't carried it anywhere since Easter Sunday, but I figured that today it might come in handy to sneak some food for Will. I was saved from further remarks by the *honk* of the Dewberry's horn.

"Don't forget the food basket. It's on the kitchen table," Mama said, as she went back to her dusting.

I handed up the food and my pocketbook to Wanda and climbed in over the tailgate of the Rambler pickup truck. I managed to wedge myself into the saved place on the seat between Wanda and Roy Lee. Our side also held one of the twins, but whether it was Sue Nell or May Belle I didn't know. Even the Dewberrys have trouble telling them apart. The seat across from us held the other twin and Sam and Pearl, who were arguing as usual. Pearl is fifteen going on sixteen, and Sam must be fourteen now, but both of them cut up as bad as the ten-year-old twins, who aren't called Double Trouble for nothing.

When I was settled, I waved through the rear window at Mr. and Mrs. Dewberry. They were up in the cab with the baby, who for some reason they all call Goober. He's only a few months old and, like most babies that age, looks exactly like Winston Churchill.

Roy Lee smiled at me but didn't say anything. He's so shy I really didn't expect him to and couldn't have heard him if he had. It isn't easy to carry on a conversation in the back of a moving pickup truck. Mr. Dewberry was really floorboarding that Rambler, bouncing us around in the back like popcorn in a hot popper. That didn't stop Wanda, who was yakking away a mile a minute. I glanced sideways at her. The kindest word for Wanda is *pudgy*, and she looked poured into her pink dress, which had been too tight when she bought it last fall.

Mr. Dewberry had turned off the highway and the deep ruts of the sandy unpaved road slowed us down considerably. Wanda poked me in the side. "Has the cat got your tongue? I've asked you three times what you think of the murder."

"Which murder?"

"*The* murder, stupid. How many murders have we had in Hines City lately?"

I didn't bother to answer—didn't have to, really, since we had reached the church by this time and Wanda was poking me again. "I wish you'd look at the preacher's message this morning."

There on the board that holds the name of the church —Shiloh Baptist, and the minister's name, Rev. Obadiah Parrish—the changeable letters spelled out, Morning Worship Service 11:00 A.M., and the motto for the day: IN SPITE OF PUBLIC OPINION, GOD'S LAST NAME IS NOT DAMN.

Giggling together, Wanda and I moved through the crowd of people who were clustered in knots outside the front church door. Homecoming Day had brought a lot of folks from Hines City and Waycross and Jacksonville and Savannah back to this yearly reunion at their mother church. Laughing, perspiring, and dressed in their Sun-

45

day best, they went around hugging and kissing and shaking hands with their kinfolks who hadn't moved away. It was bedlam. Hands kept reaching out to tug at me, old friends sending messages to my parents. I *yes ma'am*ed and *yes sir*ed my way to the shade of a live oak tree where Wanda was standing, her black eyes darting from one boy's face to another.

Out of the babble that reached my ears, the loudest voices were those of members of the posse who had traded off with other men and taken time out from their tracking in order to come to church. The words would have been loud and clear, except Wanda was mouthing something idiotic about topless bathing suits. It was like listening to two stations coming in together on a radio without a fine tuner.

One of the men was saying, "Ain't no doubt but we'll round him up. It's just takin' a little longer than we'd expected."

And Wanda was making a point, "Well, even if I had the nerve to wear one, Hines City's so backwoods and hick-town, the stores no doubt won't have them in stock until the year two thousand. And the deacons and other old fogeys would probably tar and feather him and ride him out of town on a rail."

"Ride who?" I asked distractedly.

"Rudi Gernreich, dopey—the guy who invented the topless bathing suit, like I told you."

"Oh Wanda, for pity's sake—won't you please be quiet?"

"Well, if you aren't something," she said, and stalked away.

Another posse member was making his statement to the whole congregation, who had by now gathered around. "It beats the hell out of me—pardon my French, ladies—how that nigger could've disappeared so fast without leaving a trace. If he's found somebody to help him, it'll go mighty hard with that person, being an accessory and all."

I was glad Wanda had left. She might be silly but she's nobody's fool, and she's always been able to practically read my mind. I closed my eyes to get rid of a sudden dizzy feeling and when I opened them there stood Wanda again. My heart kept sinking to the bottom of my Sunday shoes, and I kept hearing that word *accessory*.

"Sandy Cason, what's the matter with you?" Wanda demanded. "You look like warmed-over death."

"Nothing. I guess it's just the heat," I said weakly, wiping my brow, which felt all cold and clammy.

"There's something on your mind," Wanda said, "and, take my word, I'll worm it out of you yet. Whatever's bugging you has to do with that posse looking for Will Brown, hasn't it?"

I didn't—I couldn't—say a word.

"Hasn't it?" Wanda repeated. "But why you'd care if they catch him or what they'll do to him beats the heck out of me. He might have been a teacher's pet and a hero back in football season, but now he's nothing but a raping murderer."

"Wanda, that's a dreadful thing to say about Will Brown—you've got no proof he's done anything wrong."

"Well," she retorted, "you've got no proof he hasn't. And if he's so doggone innocent, why is he running and hiding?"

I whirled away from her, knowing I had to be super careful or Wanda would trip me up. Praise be, I was saved for the moment when the church doors opened and everyone filed inside.

Reverend Parrish is not the sort to pass up an opportunity to preach about a real live murder instead of the usual everyday sins, and I could sense him getting ready like a runner before a race. As part of the warming up exercises, he had us open the singing with "Onward, Christian Soldiers." The congregation struggled to keep up with Miss Sadie Cohen who was pumping away at the organ as though seeing just how fast she could play.

There's nothing Miss Cohen likes better than a really spirited hymn. She looked even more pleased with the second song, which was louder and faster than the first, and her gray head bobbed up and down happily each time she stomped the pedals of her organ. I guess technically it belongs to the church, but nobody ever calls it anything but Miss Sadie Cohen's organ. I think Miss Cohen converted to Baptist—years ago, before my time—just to play that organ. But it might have been simply because there isn't a synagogue within a good fifty miles. Jews are even scarcer around here than Episcopalians and Catholics.

As the last note of "Lead On, O King Eternal" shook the stained glass window and finally died away, Reverend Parrish announced his text, "Thou Shalt Not Kill," in such a loud and booming voice that Wanda jabbed me with her elbow and whispered, "Who does he think he is, Moses in a bow tie?" Ordinarily, I would have giggled with her, but there was nothing ordinary about this day. I slid down deeper in the pew and prayed that no matter what the preacher said I could keep my face blank until the service was over.

I willed myself not to listen but phrases—ugly and hateful—kept breaking through: *cursed is the slayer of the innocent—cut down in the flower of her youth—carnal lust—black son of Cain—aboriginal mind—*

I was worn to a nubbin when we rose for the benediction.

Outside, the congregation, quieter and more subdued, followed the usual pattern. The men gathered to one side to talk and smoke cigarettes while the women busied themselves unloading the picnic baskets, piling mountains of food on the long plank tables that stood in a grove of trees.

Most of the people present ate like they'd never had a decent meal, so I don't think they noticed I made a half dozen trips to the loaded tables. Every time Wanda hopped up to run back for extra helpings, I could count on her stopping to flirt with one or two boys. And each time she did, I chose the ungooiest food I could find and crammed it in my pocketbook for Will. I finally had it filled with drumsticks, slices of cake, a roll wrapped around some barbecued beef, two of Mama's deviled eggs, and a piece of pecan pie. I fastened the catch. Now all I had to do was get home without its springing open.

CHAPTER 6

Most any other time, the Dewberrys would simply have dropped me off and gone on their way, but Mama and Papa both were sitting on our front porch when we drove up. Nothing would do but for the Dewberrys to all pile out to greet Papa. In the confusion, I slipped inside and hid Will's food in the bottom of my closet.

When I came outside, Mrs. Dewberry was waving her hands in the air to illustrate to Mama some of the gossip she'd carted home from church; Sam was blowing bubble gum with loud smacking noises and rocking away in the chair he'd managed to grab; and Pearl, who had managed to grab another, was staring in a compact mirror and plucking her scanty eyebrows with her thumb and middle finger. From the bottom step, the Gruesome Twosome were making monster faces at each other. Mrs. Dewberry flapped a hand in their direction, "Stop that, May Belle, Sue Nell. You're gonna unhinge your jaws and pop your eyes clean out of their sockets."

Wanda was leaning against the wall pouting because I wouldn't go inside and play records.

"I can't, that's all," I said, not looking up from where I sat cross-legged on the floor.

"That's not very polite—I'm company and you're supposed to entertain me."

"Well, I can't right now," I repeated.

She flounced over to perch on the railing, throwing dirty looks in my direction. I couldn't explain that I had to stay outside to count noses. I wouldn't put it past Sam, or Pearl, or both to disappear around back for a cigarette. Sam's been smoking as long as I can remember, but it sure hasn't stunted his growth. He's lardy fat and nearly six feet tall.

I'd decided that if any of the kids even looked in the direction of the swamp or got it in their heads to wander off in that direction, I'd pretend a fainting fit. I was getting awfully jittery and wished with all my heart that the whole shooting match would pack up their things and leave. I wanted—I really needed—to go see about Will, and here I was stuck with this invasion of clowns. The only one who acted like he had a grain of sense was Roy Lee. He was leaning against a post next to me, whittling on a small chunk of wood. He's always carving little animals and birds out of walnut or cedar. I could tell by the bushy tail that this would turn out to be a standing squirrel.

Of all the Dewberry kids, Roy Lee is by far the nicest. Half the girls in junior high have a crush on him. Even though he's just thirteen, he's the smartest boy in school, but Lord he's shy. The only thing he really comes out of his shell for is baseball. He eats, breathes, and sleeps it, and you never see him without his baseball cap, winter or summer. Lately it seems he's coming out of his shyness a little, but he still has a long way to go.

It was like watching a volleyball match. At one end of the porch, Papa and Mr. Dewberry were taking President LBJ apart, and at the other, Mrs. Dewberry was saying to

51

Mama, "I have no faith in the Pill. When Ernest and I first got married, we tried the rhythm method, and the first two younguns came out jitterbugging, so we decided to just let nature take its course." She laughed loudly, and Mama tried to smile, but I could see she had missed the point if there had been one.

Then, although I knew it was bound to come sooner or later, I still wasn't prepared for their talk to turn to the murder. I had hoped they'd let that topic alone, but they pounced upon it all at once and the porch grew quiet.

"Tom, what do *you* think?" Mr. Dewberry was asking Papa. "You reckon that nigger really killed that woman?"

Mama winced at the use of that forbidden word *nigger*.

"Well, I'll tell you, Ernest," Papa replied slowly, "I don't know a whole heap about it except what I've heard on the news. But I've got my doubts. From what I know of the Adams woman, it could have been anybody, starting with her husband. The boy probably didn't do it. But if he didn't, I can't figure out why he ran away like he did."

"That beats me, too," Mrs. Dewberry squeaked. "It fails to make any sense at all. Why didn't he just stay put and tell 'em he didn't do it?"

I sat there all tensed up, biting my tongue to keep from telling them why.

Sam chimed in, "How can you tell what's going on in their heads? Most of them act like they ain't all there."

That was too much for Papa. He said in an easy voice, but with enough authority to silence that idiot Sam, "That's where you're wrong. A lot of Negroes have extremely high IQ's. Take George Washington Carver or Ralph Bunche, for example. Or Martin Luther King."

"That's the white blood in 'em, I suspect," Mr. Dewberry said.

"Could be," Papa said agreeably, "but I doubt it. I think, all in all, the black race has just as much sense as the majority of whites I know."

Mama interrupted, "You're right, Tom—my dear Aunt Polly was a fountain of wisdom. She never saw the inside of a schoolroom, but she had more sense in her little finger than most folks have in their head." She took a sighing breath. "But I'm afraid her sort is dying out and things are changing so fast."

I was listening hard to every word. As long as I can remember, there'd been this kind of grown-up talk in the background—like a giant checkerboard: white against black—but I'd paid no more attention than I had to discussions of crops or politics or religion.

"Well, the way I see it," Papa was saying, "it's more or less a matter of bad timing. We're being pushed too far too fast too soon." He paused, choosing his words. "I guess I'm just a typical slow-moving Southerner. I hate to be pressured, and I'll fight when I'm backed into a corner. That's what started all the ruckus up in Mississippi and Alabama, and God knows there's nobody winning up there. I'd hate to see that kind of violence here in Georgia, but it could happen at any time."

About that time Goober let out a yell from where he'd been sleeping on a makeshift pallet by his mother's rocker. Running an expert hand inside the rim of his diaper, Mrs. Dewberry announced, "Drenched again. Pearl, come over here and change your little brother. You're better at stooping than me." Raising her voice to carry the length of the porch, she called out to Papa, "Say, Tom, didja know we've changed the baby's name to Liberace?"

"No, Sal," Papa replied good-naturedly. "What made you do that?"

"We call him Liberace because he's the pianist."

Mama looked blank and Mrs. Dewberry tried to explain. "Pianist—get it? Peein'-est."

Mama still looked blank. I groaned and thought of a few of the words Mama had used off and on through the years to describe the Dewberry family—*coarse* and *country* and *common*. I agreed with every one of them. If only they'd get up and leave. And then, like a modern day miracle, they did.

With weary sighs of relief, my parents went to their room for their usual Sunday nap. Inside my own bedroom, I hastily changed clothes and transferred Will's food to a shopping bag. I needed the extra room to hold one of Papa's flashlights and my transistor radio and headphones. I was going to miss my radio. It was almost like parting with a piece of me, but now that I had taken on Will as my responsibility, anything that would give him a small amount of comfort was bound to make me feel a little easier. I also poked in a couple of plastic bottles of Papa's leftover pills from the kitchen shelf where they were kept. He wouldn't be needing them now that he was all through taking medicine, and maybe Mama wouldn't miss them.

Inside the tree house, I flopped on the edge of the lumpy bed, which Will had tried his best to straighten. Will was sitting on the floor across from me, his bad leg sticking straight out in front. He looked uncomfortable. I *felt* uncomfortable. I don't know why it is, but each time I went to the tree house, for the first few minutes we were like a couple of bantam chickens circling around a barnyard, sizing each other up. It takes a while for us to warm up to each other.

I fished around in the shopping bag and handed him

54

the stuff I'd brought. Will just sat there, passing the radio from hand to hand. Then he looked at me. "I'll take good care of it, Sandy. You can count on that."

"I'm not worried about it. And besides, I've got another one at home." There I was, lying again. I don't think there's any hope for me ever getting to Heaven.

I rummaged around in the bottom of the bag and came up with the plastic bottles of medicine. "Here, take these. Maybe they'll help your leg. One says Penicillin, and the other says Every four hours for pain. If you start on them right away, you're bound to be better in a couple of days."

Will slumped against the wall. "Let's hope. If not, I might as well turn myself in."

I didn't know what to say to him. In silence, I got up and looked through the crack. The swamp made a green and gray world around us. Tatters of wispy moss were trailing from every cypress limb and a young pond gannet stood motionless between the cypress knees, its feathers silvered by the fading light.

"There's no place in the whole wide world like the swamp," I said.

"You're right, Sandy, but don't let anyone tell you a swamp goes to sleep at night. I never heard so many strange noises—really weird. I keep thinking about what Uncle Pete says, that these old woods used to be full of bears and bobcats and there's bound to be some of them left." He gave me that funny grin I was used to now. "But I'd a heap rather tangle with them than Sheriff Wiggins and the posse."

"Don't joke about it, Will," I begged.

"Who's joking? Nobody has to tell me this ain't no laughing matter."

I deliberately changed the subject. "What about your

family, Will? You haven't said much about them."

He shrugged. "There's not much to tell. Besides, we're so scattered now, there's hardly a family left. It's dwindled down to me and Uncle Pete at home, since my littlest brother and sister have gone to live with an aunt in Savannah." Leaning his head back against the tree house wall, he half closed his eyes, thinking. "There used to be five of us kids. I was sort of the middle one, the one most apt to get lost in the shuffle. My daddy's name was Edward Brown—Big Ed, they called him. He was a real roadrunner and left home for good right after my baby sister Lottie came along. Ma managed somehow to keep us together, but after a while I guess she got worn out with trying. It's been catch-as-catch-can since Ma gave up and died." There was no mistaking the love in his voice. "My Ma was really something. If there was a market for pride, we'd a been as rich as the Kennedys. No welfare checks or government handouts for Ma. By working from sunup to sundown, she kept us all going, and I never heard her grumble, not one single time."

"Tell me about Big Bubba, the one you'll be living with when you get down to Florida."

"That old boy is like nothing you every saw. Big Bubba and I are like two crossed fingers—close together but pointing in different directions. We get along fine." He shifted his position and I could tell his leg was hurting again. He kept on talking. "Big Bubba's got no education to speak of, but he's smart as a whip. When I first started cleaning Mrs. Adams' yards a couple of years ago, Big Bubba told me right off that she was strictly a no-good woman and I was headed for trouble. So what did I do? Like a moron I ignored him and kept on working for her. From the start she acted mighty peculiar—she treated me like I was blind."

He paused for a moment and I thought that was all he was planning to say, but then he started talking again, not really to me but more like thinking aloud. "She'd parade herself all over that big backyard with the high fence around it. Thank God there was a fence so the neighbors couldn't see in, 'cause half the time she'd have next to nothing on. She'd follow me so close she'd practically step on the rake and she'd say, 'Hot, ain't it?' and I'd say, 'Yes'm,' and I'd rake like the devil was behind me. And then she'd say, 'Ain't you got no manners, boy? I spoke to you,' and I'd say 'Yes'm,' and then she'd stretch her arms up and lift that yellow white hair from her neck and she'd say, 'My, but it's hotter'n the hinges of hell. Far too hot for rakin'. Would you like to come in the kitchen for a drink of water or a Coke?' and I'd say, 'No'm,' as polite as I could although by that time my tongue was stuck to the roof of my mouth."

I clamped my hands over my ears and begged, "Please don't, Will."

Will's eyes opened wide in surprise. "What's the matter, am I shocking you?"

"No, you're scaring me. You're making that woman come alive."

"Sandy," Will said slowly, "that woman was real and she was very much alive, and now she's dead. This isn't some game we're playing,"

"I know," I said miserably. Then, breaking an awkward silence, I added, "I'm sorry I interrupted. Tell me about the rest of your family."

Will lifted his shoulders in another shrug. "Like I said, there's nothing to tell."

"Please. Tell me about your sister. Not the baby, the oldest one."

With a little laugh, Will said, "There's no way to de-

57

scribe Hessie—the Lord tore up the mold when He finished making her. She was always my favorite in the family, but after Ma died, there wasn't no holding her in Hines City."

"Where did she go?"

"I don't know for sure, but I've got a sneaking feeling she's with the freedom riders somewhere in Alabama. Ever since she first drew breath, she's been trying to change the world. I tried to tell her—we all tried to tell her—she was fixing to get in a peck of trouble, but she's the kind that never allowed herself to listen. I sure do miss her." After a pause, Will added, "But, come to think of it, it's just as well she's not here now, with me in all this mess. Knowing Hessie, she'd probably be trailing after the posse to give them a piece of her mind. I wouldn't put it past her to tangle with the Ku Klux Klan."

"The what?"

"Nothing. Just forget I said that, OK?"

"But I heard what you said. You said the Ku Klux Klan."

"Well, what if I did? I'm sure you've heard of it before."

"In a way," I admitted, "but what little I've heard doesn't make much sense. And I doubt your sister would find anything like that down here in south Georgia."

"Don't bet any money on it. From what I hear, the Klan is springing up all over the place. They're not all over in Mississippi killing off civil rights workers. Or don't you remember last year when Klansmen shot those three students and covered them with a bulldozer."

I shivered. "Stop it, Will Brown—that's scary and gruesome. Besides, it's hundreds of miles to Mississippi."

"You're right, Sandy—I'm sorry. And you're probably

right about there not being a group of KKK in Hines County," Will said, but he didn't sound too convincing.

I reached for the radio and turned it on low. "Here, find yourself some Elvis Presley and think about something cheerful. It's time for me to be going."

Will lifted his hand in a good-bye motion and then he turned his palm to point out the things I'd brought to him. "I'm not much with words, but I'm much obliged to you, Sandy, for all this stuff. Lord knows what I would have done if you hadn't come—starved to death, for the main thing. Someday I'll pay you back."

"Forget it, Will. You don't owe me anything," I said, escaping through the door.

CHAPTER 7

I had nightmares all night long, which got my sleeping and waking pretty well mixed up. I was tempted once or twice to go crawl in the bed with Mama and Papa like I used to when I was little and they could sandwich me in between them without any problem. But I decided against it. One of the bad things about growing up is that you take up so darned much space in a bed.

The *hrrmph hrrmph* of Lester O'Kelly's motorcycle at two or three in the morning didn't help my sleeping. I could hear him and Pearl Dewberry squealing as they roared down the road. Mama would kill me—hack me in little pieces—if I turned out to be as crazy as Pearl. Pearl's so hung up on sex that if it came packaged like sugar, she'd sprinkle it on her cereal in the mornings. But she's really asking for trouble hanging out with Lester. He's a flat-out moron.

In the silence they left behind them, I thought about Will again. That made me think of the Ku Klux Klan, which is probably why I had the bad dreams to begin with. I fished around in my mind for all I knew about the KKK and came up with practically nothing. And what little I'd heard made the Klan seem like a bunch of bogeymen—make-believe characters to scare little kids or something. On the TV news from Mississippi and Alabama and other places way off, the men of the Klan stayed hidden behind their masks and wrapped in their long white robes and didn't seem like men at all.

I turned on my bedside lamp and tossed the top sheet aside. In bare feet, I crossed over to my desk and looked on the shelf Papa had built above it. Pulling down the J-K volume of the *World Book Encyclopedia*, I leafed through Krypton and Kshatriya and Ku K'ai-chih and there it was—Ku Klux Klan. The photograph was scary enough: members of the Klan wearing white robes and hoods and burning a fiery cross. But the printed words were even scarier. They traced the story of the KKK from its beginning in Reconstruction days and ended up by saying that, after World War II, the Klan had started up again in practically every Southern state, including Georgia and Florida. Like a blow it came to me that Will could be right. There might be a KKK closer than I had thought.

Suddenly chilled, I closed the encyclopedia and hurried back to my bed. Stretched out again, I picked up my history book and, all on its own, it fell open at the Gettysburg Address.

I tried to read but the words ran together, making practically no sense, and suddenly I wished Miss Everett had never come up with the bright idea of tying our Commencement program in with the Civil War Centennial. By the time I reached the part that says *The brave men, living and dead, who struggled here, have consecrated it, far above our poor power to add or detract*, my eyes were gluing together, and the next thing I knew the sun was shining.

I dressed in slow motion since, thanks to a district

teachers' meeting, there was no school today. There certainly wasn't any rush to get over to the Dewberrys' house to visit Wanda. I didn't really want to go, but I had promised.

I took a shortcut through the edge of the woods, which brought me out at the back of the Dewberry house. There wasn't a soul in sight, so I walked around to the front where Wanda, tousle haired and sleepy eyed, sat in the front porch swing. Her greeting to me was a casual wave of her hand toward a large porch rocker.

Wanda continued to pick at a scabby mosquito bite on her ankle, completely ignoring me. Then, looking in my direction, she asked, "What's the matter with you this morning? Have you swallowed your tongue?"

"Nothing's the matter with me. I'm just not in a talking mood." I patiently waited for Wanda to open the conversation. Like all the Dewberrys except Roy Lee, she never runs out of things to talk about. It took her only a second to come up with something.

"I wonder if the posse's caught up with that murdering nigger, Will Brown?"

"He's not a nigger and he's not a murderer," I said, before I could catch myself. I almost died where I sat because Wanda isn't stupid. She sat there with her mouth hanging open and stared at me. I tried to cover up in a hurry. "You know how I hate that word, *nigger*. It sounds so, I dunno, so ugly."

Wanda shrugged. "It's just a word. Who cares?" She looked at me hard. "Sometimes I get the feeling you're color-blind. You treat the ones in our class like they're as white as us. You've even made friends with some," she added, accusing me. "But that's beside the point. I don't give a rip if you call Will Brown a black or a Nigra or an

Afro-American. What makes you think he's not the one who murdered Mrs. Adams? Everybody in Hines County knows he did it. Why else would he run away?'"

"Maybe he was scared."

"Of course he was scared. I'd be scared, too, if I murdered somebody in cold blood. But you still haven't answered question number one: What makes you think Will Brown didn't kill that woman? You sound like you know something you're not telling."

I managed to stammer out, "There's just no way he could have been the person who killed her. No way. He isn't but seventeen or maybe eighteen, and he used to hunt and fish with Benjie, and you know he was an honor student, and the star on the football team—" My voice trailed off into miserable silence. It sounded mighty feeble to me.

"What's that got to do with anything? Maybe, like the stories in *True Detective*, it was a crime of passion." She got up and sauntered around the end of the porch, sticking out her chest and wiggling her hips. "Maybe she kept on teasin' him and got him all steamed up and maybe he didn't take time to think and—"

"You're crazy, Wanda Dewberry," I interrupted. "You might think you know what you're talkng about, but you don't."

"I know one thing," Wanda said calmly, sitting back down in the swing, and her voice made little goose bumps run all over me, "you know something I don't know, but I'll figure it out. You just wait and see."

"There's nothing to figure out." I tried to sound positive and sure, but I felt all squished and soggy.

I'd never dreamed I'd ever welcome Sam Dewberry but when he appeared on the porch, I felt like a drowning girl being pulled from some very deep water.

Grunting a little with all his extra fat, Sam squatted down on the floor, halfway between me and Wanda. After a quick check to make sure there was no other Dewberry lurking around, he pulled out a crumpled pack of Camels and got one going. "I might be a fool for asking, but can you girls keep a secret?"

"What kind of secret?" Wanda demanded.

"A real big honest-to-Pete kind of secret."

"I doubt if it's all that big," said Wanda, "but, sure, we'll keep your secret."

Sam leaned forward and lowered his voice, "Well, I hitched a ride to town this mornin' and I found out some very interesting news."

Roy Lee rounded the house and walked up on the porch, giving all three of us a curious look. "Am I interrupting something?"

Sam considered a moment. "Naw, you might as well hear it, too. Well, what I found out is the Ku Klux Klan is meetin' Thursday night down in that piece of pasture near the Willett place." He gave a furtive look around and dropped his voice even lower. "The four of us could slip down there real easy and watch 'em hold their meetin'— they might even burn a cross or somethin'."

"You're making this up," I gasped, feeling a stab of terror.

Even Wanda looked startled. "Sam, I know you're batty as a bedbug, but even so—" For once, she was practically speechless. Recovering, she said, "In the first place, how would you know? Who in their right mind would tell *you* a thing like that?"

Sam gave us a superior look. "Never mind how I know —the point I'm tryin' to make is whether or not you're game to hide down there and see what they're up to."

His words were barely making sense to me. My thoughts had flown to Will in the tree house, and I felt trapped and helpless. If Sam was right, Will was in danger not only from the posse, but maybe from the Klan as well. One or the other was bound to find his hiding place.

Roy Lee was asking Sam, "Why tell us about it? You too scared to go there by yourself, or you just want our company?"

Sam balled up his fist and bared his Camel-colored teeth. "I ain't scared of nothin' and you know it, Roy Lee. You don't even know when I'm tryin' to be nice and friendly."

"Well, that happens so seldom, you can't blame us for not catching on right away," Wanda said sarcastically.

"I think your idea's crazy—plain old crazy." I swallowed. "In the first place, I don't believe there is a Ku Klux Klan in Hines County and, second of all, even if there was, Mama and Papa would skin me alive before they'd let me go anywhere near them."

"Well, I hope you got enough sense not to ask your parents," Sam snarled. "Why can't you tell 'em you're spendin' the night with Wanda?"

"Thursday's a school night." Even to me that sounded like a flimsy excuse. There's never any homework during the last few days of school and, with finals over, nobody ever cracks a book.

"Plus, Mr. Know-it-all," Wanda asked Sam, "what do you plan to tell *our* folks? Even they would draw the line at letting us spy on the Ku Klux Klan. Pa won't even let us mention the Klan."

"That's easy," Sam replied smugly. "We'll tell' em we're goin' bullfrog giggin' down at Sawmill Pond."

"You all count me out," I said. "I think it's the worst

idea I've ever heard, and I don't mind admitting I'm scared. I'd be scared plumb skinny to do a thing like that."

Roy Lee put his head close to my chair and practically whispered, "I don't blame you, Sandy. But if you change your mind, I'll try to look out for you."

I studied Roy Lee's face for a moment, and then backed down a little. "Let me think about it and then I'll decide—I'll call you and let you know."

Sam exploded. "Look, ninny, don't say a word on the phone about any of this. You'll get us all in a heap of trouble."

"OK, OK, take it easy—I'll tell you at school tomorrow." I got to my feet. "Right now I better get on home."

CHAPTER 8

When I got home, I could see Papa stretched out in his recliner in front of the TV set. He must have been napping since the screen showed nothing but rolling horizontal lines. Mama had returned from the Hines County Courthouse, where she had spent the morning. She was at the dining room table with her DAR papers and notebooks spread all around the file box where she keeps her ancestors buried in alphabetical order. When I was a little kid, Mama wasted her breath warning me not to play with her files. I wouldn't have opened that drawer for anything, for fear all those musty and mildewed dead cousins and great-aunts might jump out.

I paused at the door. "Mama, I'll see you later. I'm going outside to play."

"Fine," replied Mama absent-mindedly, not looking up from her files.

Quickly and quietly, I gathered up food from the kitchen—mostly odds and ends that wouldn't be missed, like doughnuts, a handful of grapes, and a small bag of jelly beans.

I had made so many trips to the tree house in the last three days I felt like a boomerang. It seemed like Will had been hiding out in the swamps forever. I could barely remember what it was like not being scared and worried.

I got no reply to my whistle. After debating a couple of seconds, I held my breath and eased the door open. When my eyes adjusted, I could see that Will was stretched out, very still and straight, on the lumpy moss bed. My heart almost stopped—I just knew that Will was dead or unconscious or something awful. But then, thank goodness, he started making little groaning noises which sounded exactly like the whimper of a real sick puppy.

"Will," I called softly. "Hey, Will—it's me, Sandy."

Will opened his eyes partway and they looked like a road map with teensy fine red lines. He moistened his lips with the tip of his tongue and managed to sit up and speak in a fuzzy voice, "Well, hey—I guess you caught me nappin'."

Walking over, I reached out my hand, like Mama's done a hundred times to me, and laid it on his forehead. He had a burning-up fever. "Will, you're sick. What did you go and get sick for?" I asked. I couldn't help it that my voice sounded angry. Now I felt more scared and helpless than ever.

Will tried to smile. "What you gettin' so mad for? You sound like an old wet hen."

"But you *are*—you're sick."

"Well, I didn't get sick on purpose. But there's no point kiddin' myself—my leg's a whole heap worse."

Not really wanting to, I looked. Will had changed the bandage but, even so, it was yellowish gray and oozy in spots. My stomach did a somersault. "When did you take your medicine?"

"I guess not since early this mornin'," Will admitted.

I didn't mean to scold but I couldn't help it. "I must say, to be as smart as you are, that's pretty dumb."

Grabbing up the empty drinking glass, I climbed down

the rickety steps to fill it with cold water from the artesian well. When I got back inside, I shook out two antibiotic capsules and a pain pill and placed them in Will's hand which was trembling like a nervous old man's. "Here, take these," I said, and watched him swallow. "This settles it, Will—we've got to get you some help. Blood poisoning can kill you."

"So can the electric chair."

"That's not very funny," I said, and my voice shook. I thought for an awful moment I was going to cry.

Will was wider awake now but still looked like warmed-over death. I heard myself repeating, "We've got to get you some help. I've been thinking, there's school again tomorrow, and maybe I can manage to find your Uncle Pete. And maybe he can come up with something." I flopped down on the floor and added, not really joking, "If nothing else, since he's not only a janitor but a preacher, maybe his praying would stand a better chance than mine of getting through to the Lord."

"That's an awful lot of *maybe*s. But I dunno—Uncle Pete's pretty smart and he's got a lot of friends, including the Lord, but I'd guess the Sheriff's got somebody watching him night and day. It would never do to connect him up with you. The posse would be out here in nothing flat."

"There's got to be an answer. I'll think of something." I stood up and motioned toward the small sack of food I'd brought. "Try to eat something—maybe some jelly beans. I ate all the licorice," I admitted. "They're my favorite."

"Well, black *is* beautiful," Will said, and I tried to smile back.

"Honestly, Will Brown—that's worse than one of Mama's jokes, and hers can be pretty gross."

Mama and Papa were already eating supper when I got back to the house. "I'm sorry I'm late," I said as I slid into my chair.

"Where on earth have you been? I called until I was blue in the face, but you didn't answer," said Mama from the foot of the table.

"I'm sorry, Mama," I repeated, suddenly realizing that I'd have to be more careful. What if Mama stopped calling from the peach orchard and set out looking for me?

Papa passed the bowl of beef stew in my direction and winked. "Well, you must admit, Laura, our daughter's like a bad penny. She always turns up."

Papa and I ate but Mama just sat there, moving a few string beans from one side of her plate to the other. Finally Papa noticed and teased her, "Hey, Laura, you're going to founder yourself if you eat all that's on your plate."

"I'm sorry, Tom, but I'm just not hungry. I guess I worked too long and hard at the courthouse today on my family records."

Papa reached for another piece of cornbread and piled on lots of butter. "Why don't you take it easy on that malarkey? It's enough to give you a running fit."

Mama sat up very straight. "I'm about to reach a stopping point. I've almost got my Bigelow line in order and I'm planning to submit it at the DAR meeting next month."

Papa shook his head. "I could understand you joining that blasted organization on the Fairchild family, Laura, if you felt you *had* to join that bunch of snobs, but why you're messing around with the Bigelows is a puzzle to me. I never knew a Bigelow yet worth the salt it would take to salt him down."

"What a dreadful thing to say," Mama spluttered.

"Honey, you know it's true. I could have said no Bigelow's worth the gunpowder it would take to blow him to hell—and I'm sure that's where they all wind up."

"Tom Cason, you're being downright hateful. You're forgetting, aren't you, that way back on my mother's side there's Bigelow blood in my veins—and in Cassandra's, too."

"Thank God, it's been well diluted," Papa replied, teasing her a little.

Mama ignored the remark and said thoughtfully, "Yes, that's the real reason I'm doing all this work on the family charts. Someday Sandy will no doubt want to know about her background. It's important to know who we are and where we come from."

"Not me," I said, "I don't give a hoot where I come from. I only want to know where I'm going. Besides, all this talk about whose blood I have running around in me makes me feel all creepy and crawly. I feel like the picture in my general science book—the one with the veins and the arteries all tangled up together."

Mama and Papa were paying no attention to me. There were times I felt shut out and a very unnecessary part of this family.

"Besides," Mama was saying, backtracking, "the ladies in the DAR are not snobs. Most of them are friendly, lovely ladies—"

"In a pig's eye," Papa interrupted. "Most of them are middle-aged idiots so hung up on family trees they put me in mind of a lynching party."

Mama pushed her plate completely away. "How can you say such things? The ladies I know are dedicated, patriotic descendants of the founders of our country."

"Bullshit," Papa said, knowing as well as I do that Mama purely despises that word. I waited for the explo-

71

sion, but to my amazement Mama laughed, and Papa reached over and placed his hand on top of hers. Mama untensed her shoulders and I slipped away from the table, completely ignored. There were times I couldn't begin to figure my parents out.

CHAPTER 9

The following morning was Tuesday, and school would be out on Friday. Just four more days to live through. That thought alone was enough to make us giddy with excitement. From the noise that ricocheted up and down the hall, it was plain that every class was bedlam.

Our homeroom teacher, Miss Everett, was trying her dead-level best to maintain some kind of order but she lost some of her cool when she found out I still hadn't memorized the Gettysburg Address.

"Sandy Cason, would you like to explain just what you've been doing with your time for the past few days?"

I practically jumped out of my skin. I could just imagine what Miss Everett would say if I told her what I really had been doing. I gave an apologetic shrug but said nothing.

She was still trying to get us to behave as she marched us in a wiggly line to the main auditorium to practice. Waving the wooden paint stirrer she carried in her hand like a flat baton, she was saying, "I've never yet used this stirrer to paddle a student but if you don't simmer down this instant—"

We laughed because none of us took her seriously. For one thing, the Board of Education has outlawed spanking, and, for another, Miss Everett's so easygoing she wouldn't hurt a fly.

Standing in the center of the stage, she cleared her throat and addressed the class, which had now found seats in the first three rows. "As you know, Friday is Commencement Day, and it's really an important day in your lives. Commencement is not only an ending of the academic year; it is also a beginning. This marks a turning point. Next year you'll be out of elementary school and starting out in junior high and then on to high school."

She paused and then ran her hand through her short curly hair. "I don't want to preach to you, but I want you to take this seriously. And this year is really important—now, in 1965, we're bringing to a close the one hundredth anniversary of the Civil War. As you all know, or should by now, the Civil War Centennial was officially begun in 1961 by an act of Congress, and the whole nation has been celebrating. No," she corrected herself, *"celebrating* is not the right word—*observing* is better—the centennial of that terrible struggle." Stepping back to the podium, she consulted her notebook. "Now, let's run through the entire program and see how it's coming along."

I sat there, lost in my own private thoughts, while the others went through their parts. And I thought that, really, I am a part of history and all of us sitting here are a part of history and the time will come when we will be gone and not even remember this day. This bright May day in 1965 will be gone forever and won't ever come back again—can't ever come back again—and history will swallow us up. And I felt very small and light and thin like the tiny sliver of sunlight that played around the ceiling of the auditorium.

Miss Everett's voice cut in, "Now, Sandy, if you'd like to come back from wherever you were, we're ready for you." But her voice was gentle and there was a brief, warm smile as she handed me her history book open to the Gettysburg Address. I felt a warm rush of love for her. I just know I'll miss her something awful when school is over.

The cafeteria was crowded at lunchtime. Hines City School is not very big, and all the grades eat together from primary on up through high school. Most of the juniors and seniors never go near the lunchroom. They'd rather settle for soft drinks and candy bars from the Zippy Mart on the corner—or even go hungry—before they'd honor us kids with their presence.

Roy Lee plunked his skimpy plateful next to mine and hooked a chair leg with his sneakered foot. "Yuk," he said, and I yukked back. He unfolded the paper napkin that diapered his knife and fork and turned to me. "They wouldn't serve slop like this at the state penitentiary in Reidsville." He swallowed a couple of bites, made a terrible face, and pushed his plate away. Leaning closer in my direction, he asked quietly, "Have you decided yet?"

I knew exactly what he meant, so I shook my head no.

"Can't say that I blame you. Like most of Sam's dumb ideas, the whole thing could turn into a real disaster." Leaning even closer, he whispered, "Think about it some more. You've still got plenty of time to make up your mind."

"My mind's made up," I said in the lowest possible voice. "I don't believe there really is a you-know-what in Hines County, but I'm not taking any chances. If I'm wrong, and they really showed up down there, it would scare me half to death—and I'm not kidding."

After Roy Lee left, I sat a little while longer and slowly became aware of snatches of conversation that rose and fell, uneven and ragged. "Yeah, my Pa's been out night and day with that posse."

"Ain't nothin' but a murderin' nigger."

"Careful, man—you bad-mouthin' one of your *equals*."

Loud, raucous laughter hurt my ears and, without really wanting to, I looked down the length of the table. Lillie Mae Crandall and Sadie Cooper, sitting close to one another like Siamese twins hastily joined together for protection, were frozen and deathly still. Unblinking eyes in their black faces looked nowhere, and only their hands, green knuckled and knotted tightly into fists, gave a clue they'd heard a word. I tried a smile in their direction, but they didn't smile back.

Suddenly I was raging mad—not everyday angry but a deep, hurting kind of anger I'd never known before. I felt like a boiling teapot without a spout, useless and deformed. Suddenly I knew without knowing how I knew that these kids weren't insulting Lillie Mae and Sadie just for the fun of it. The world wasn't hunting Will Brown down like an animal because some idiot woman named Mrs. Adams had got herself strangled in a bathtub. The real reason was bigger than that, older than that, and certainly older and bigger than me. I sat there hating myself for being only twelve and nowhere near smart enough to figure it out.

Afternoon recess was my only chance to look for Will's Uncle Pete. Standing at the grimy white outside fountain, I pretended to drink from the lukewarm trickle of water while my eyes scanned the school grounds. Nothing. And nobody. He could be anywhere, even the shop or gymnasium.

I sidled away from the fountain and, avoiding as many kids as I could, I moved around the corner of the building and headed for the covered walkways that connect the elementary school with the junior high and high school. At the entrance to the upper class buildings, I stopped. I'd run errands over there before and been there once or twice with Benjie, but this was my first time strictly on my own.

But then, as I started to enter, I saw him on the grounds, poking heaped-up trash from metal wastebaskets into the open jaws of the Dempster Dumpster. It had to be Will's Uncle Pete—a tall, thin elderly man in olive green coveralls. Gold-rimmed spectacles were perched on the bridge of a long straight nose and gleamed against the mahogany brown of his face.

Quickly now, I half walked, half ran over to where he stood, still and straight, questioning me with his eyes. Immediately I was in trouble, for I didn't know his last name. Since he was Will's uncle on his mother's side, his last name wouldn't be Brown—and I couldn't just call him Uncle Pete and, goodness knows, Preacher Pete sounded ridiculous. So I didn't call him anything. I simply asked before I lost my nerve, "Sir, are you Will Brown's uncle?"

He looked at me, hard and searching, as though he was making up his mind about something. Finally he replied, "Yes, missy, I'm Peter Hawkins, and Will's my sister's child. Do you mind me askin' why you want to know?"

I gulped and said, "Well, sir, it's just that I know where Will is hiding out. When he was running away Friday night, he hurt his leg real bad. He's in my tree house in the swamps about five miles from here."

A mixture of emotions garbled up his face as he reached out a long thin hand and grabbed my shoulder. "Go on, child—tell me all you know about Will."

In my race with the recess bell, my words ran together

as I covered the last three days. When I came to a stop, there were tears on Mr. Hawkin's face, leaking ever so slowly down the creases by the side of his nose and dropping on the front of his coveralls. "Praise the Lord—praise be to the Heavenly Father," he said, and then let go of my shoulder.

The bell was ringing, drowning out my words, but I held up my hand when the shrill tinny sound died away. "By the way, sir, Will told me to tell you—to make it real plain—that you're not to do anything now." I ticked off Will's instructions on my fingers. "First, don't try to come to see him—you'd lead the posse straight to his hiding place. And second, you're not to tell a soul, not a living soul—not a neighbor, not your friends in your lodge, not a one of the smaller children—nobody."

"I understand. But would you pass on a message for me? Would you tell him he's never been out of my prayers, and I ain't the only one knowin' he's innocent, and I'm sendin' my steadfast love to keep him company." After a pause, he added, almost to himself, "And tell him to hang on to his faith—the Almighty God will give him comfort and find a way to deliver him out of his trials and tribulations."

"Yes, sir," I promised. I whirled around, tossing my parting words over my shoulder, "Bye, sir, I'll see you same place, same time tomorrow."

In the classroom, all eyes turned in my direction as I slid into my seat, trying to calm my breathing. Miss Everett eyed me silently, then walked from her desk to mine. Leaning down, she whispered, "Sandy, honey, is there anything wrong? You're looking and behaving in a most peculiar way."

"No, ma'am, I'm fine," was all I could come up with.

78

CHAPTER 10

When I got home from school, Mama was sitting, stiff jointed and straight, in the antique velvet rocker in the corner of the living room. She could have almost been one of the photographs from the flat red family album she held in her lap. Her hands were folded tightly and she wasn't turning the pages. As far as I could tell, she wasn't doing anything but staring off into some distant place.

"Hi, Mama, I'm home. I think I'll go outside and play for a little bit," which meant, of course, that I had to go check on Will.

"Fine, dear," Mama said, laying the heavy album on the marble-topped table. "I baked some brownies today. Why don't you go sample them? I think I'll lie down for a little nap."

"Thanks, Mama." Then, from the door, I turned back to her. "Are you OK?"

"I'm fine," she said, but her face had a mournful far-away look which made me want to go over and give her a hug and a kiss, but of course I didn't. It might be mine but it isn't Mama's way of showing love.

In the kitchen, I picked up a brownie and ate it quickly,

washing it down with a glass of cold milk. Then I wrapped up four of the brownies in a piece of Saran Wrap and fixed a baloney sandwich for Will. After debating a moment, I decided on a frozen can of lemonade to mix with the water flowing from the artesian well.

Will's answer to my whistle came immediately; he'd been waiting for me. How awful it must be to stay shut up in that little space all night and all day with nothing to do but listen to a radio and worry and wait.

"Hi, Sandy," Will said when I stepped inside. His voice was eager and friendly, and I was relieved. Maybe we'd reached a point where we could cut out all that sparring around every time we met.

He wasn't limping nearly as bad as he crossed the room and the pain lines were practically gone from his face. "Hey, that's great," I said. "Your leg must be a whole heap better."

"I'm afraid to count on it, but I think it is."

I handed him the little bag of food. "Here, don't you want to eat?"

"Not now." He shook his head impatiently. "What I'm hungry for is news of Uncle Pete. Did you see him?"

Carefully, trying to remember every single thing, I told Will all about it. When I had finished, he made me tell it all through again.

Taking my usual seat on the edge of the lumpy bed, I glanced over at Will. He sat in his place with an empty, faraway look on his face that made me realize how homesick he must be. Quietly, trying not to disturb him, I picked up the almost empty Mason jar, dashed the stale water through the window crack, and took the jar with me down to the well. I stood watching the water overflowing the trough. The fuzzy pale green moss that clung to the hollowed-out wood moved lazily inside. In the damp ground around the edges, the water fern curled its fronds above the tiny little flowers of the arum and wild calla and the hooded cup of the flycatcher plant.

Papa had taught me the names of everything in the swamp. One big question mark, that's what he always called me. When the fish weren't biting, we'd make a game of collecting the different plants that grew in the shallow water. I took them home to press them, next to their descriptions, in the huge old unabridged dictionary. Papa, in one of his weaker moments, or so he said, had bought it from a traveling salesman. As far as I know, our plants are still hidden there—tissue thin and faded. And I can remember copying the definitions to study later— big words with backward Ss and wobbly Ts—and Papa would gather me close and smile. "You're learning, Sandy—you're learning." But now, when I really needed answers to big important questions, I couldn't turn to Papa. All I could do was stand in this cool green magic place, feeling strangely sad and lonely.

Giving myself a shake to come to, I carefully climbed the pegs with the too-full Mason jar sloshing with every step.

"I thought I'd lost you, Sandy," said Will, watching as I stirred the melting lemonade in the water. I handed him a glass and sat back down.

Will took long, big swallows and set his glass aside. "Super," he said, with an exaggerated *smack*. Then, cocking his head to one side, he gave me a questioning look. "Sandy, what's eatin' on you? Your mind off in space somewhere?"

"I guess it is," I mumbled. Was it showing—how confused and scared I felt? I really couldn't tell. All I knew for sure was that I felt weighted down with questions I couldn't find an answer to, things I felt too stupid to cope with. That's the word, *cope*. I'd never really known the meaning before.

"Come on, tell me. What's bugging you?" Will asked.

"How's your medicine holding out?" I asked. Answering a question with a question is a trick of mine that sends Mama straight up the wall.

Outside the tree house, the clouds were swollen with rain and the sky was growing darker. Off in the distance there were sudden flashes of heat lightning and the rumbling sound of thunder. Common sense told me I ought to go before the rain started or I might get soaking wet. That would be a little hard to explain. But the tree house seemed so cozy, in spite of the cracks.

Another big boom of thunder rattled around us. When it died away, Will looked over at me. "Uncle Pete says that back in the old days, when folks heard thunder they swore it was the Devil beating his wife."

The old days made me think of Mama again.

"Will, do you ever wonder what it was like back then?"

"Back when?"

"Back in plantation days, when all this land"—I spread my hands wide—"was covered with cotton fields and big old tobacco farms and hundreds of people lived out here in the country."

"Yeah, I sometimes wonder, especially if you mean back in slavery days." Will's face was blank, and I wanted to change the subject, but somehow I couldn't.

My silly words kept pouring out. "The way Mama makes it sound is that it used to be paradise, with parties and dressed-up ladies and scads of money and—" My voice trailed away.

"Well, Sandy," Will said calmly, "it might have been heaven on earth for those folks drinkin' mint juleps on

82

the veranda, but from what I hear it was hell for those out choppin' the cotton."

I stumbled on, with questions springing up out of nowhere. "Do you ever get angry with me because my people owned—" I stopped.

"Because *your* people owned *my* people?" Will finished up for me. He closed his eyes for a moment, those thick lashes fanning his high cheekbones. Then he opened his eyes, and I could tell he was choosing his words: "Yeah, I guess in a general way I do. Not you, exactly, but all white people. Blacks have a long memory, and they've got an awful lot to remember. Stories are handed down from generation to generation—"

"Like Mama's family heirlooms," I said in a small voice, but I don't think Will even heard me.

He was saying, "Some of those stories are enough to curl your hair. Maybe that's why most of us are born like this—" he said, half joking, as he laid his hand on the crown of his head.

"But, Will, I didn't—" Again I stopped. I was trying to defend myself, but from what I wasn't quite sure.

"I know," said Will in a soothing voice. "You didn't invent slavery; you didn't set up the system. You're right about that—it wasn't your fault. Any more than it was mine. I guess the question now, in 1965, is what we're gonna do about it."

This conversation was certainly taking a strange turn. But, on the other hand, this was the first time Will and I had ever talked—really talked, that is. Sure, we'd exchanged messages and said a few words now and then, but we hadn't talked together.

I rose to my feet. "I'll see you tomorrow. Is there anything you want me to tell Uncle Pete?"

Will thought for a moment. "You can tell him not to worry." Then he added in a low but not embarrassed voice, "And tell him I love him a lot, and *please* not to worry."

Fat raindrops were *plunk*ing *ker-plunk*ing down, spattering against my cheeks and the top of my head as I ran back home. Mostly dry, I fastened the screen door behind me as the clouds opened up.

Mama was still in her bedroom and Papa had not come home, so I went to my room and pressed my nose against the cold windowpane fogged over by the rain, staring into nothing. When at last the rain stopped, I wandered out to the porch. Drying off my favorite rocking chair with the palm of my hand, I sat and watched the sun break through the clouds.

I was still sitting there when Roy Lee appeared on his bike.

Both of us rocked for a while, not saying much of anything. Roy Lee was whittling. He was putting the finishing touches on a standing squirrel which, tiny as it was, looked almost alive in his hands. I wanted to reach out and touch the little bushy tail and the small front paws, which were holding a miniature acorn.

Roy Lee folded his knife, pocketed it, and thrust the carving out to me. "Here, take it—it's yours."

"Who, me? Why me?" I sounded like a perfect idiot.

"Why not?" Roy Lee's face beneath his baseball cap turned faintly pink, but he was smiling.

"Well, gee whiz, thanks. Thanks a whole heap." I cupped the squirrel in my hand and stared at little eyes which were so real they seemed to stare back at me in a friendly way. "I don't know how you do it," I said. "I really don't."

"It's nothing," Roy Lee said. Then turning to me, he asked abruptly, "Tell me, what have you decided to do about Thursday night?"

Before I could stop to think, I heard myself replying, "I've decided to go." The words were out, heavy and scary, but I didn't take them back.

CHAPTER 11

Next day, at afternoon recess, Uncle Pete was waiting by the Dempster Dumpster, standing quiet and motionless like a man who is used to waiting. I gave him what little news I had about Will, wishing I could stretch it out to sound more hopeful and cheerful instead of so bare and pitiful. He listened without any expression on his face, not a twitch or a ripple, until his eyes filled up when I gave him Will's brief message about sending his love.

"The Almighty tore up the mold when He made that boy," he said when I finished. "How the people in this town—how anybody who knowed him personal—could think he'd harm a living creature is more than I can fathom." He was rubbing his hands together in a washing motion.

"I know, sir," I replied, hoping to soothe him. "We both know that Will's not a murderer." The word *murderer* made him wring his hands even faster and I could have bitten my tongue. There was something about saying it out loud that made the whole thing more of a nightmare.

We just stood looking at one another, for what was beginning to seem an awful long time. Suddenly the recess bell rang out, tinny and businesslike, and I could safely leave. As I turned to go, Uncle Pete held out his hand, and in his gray pink palm there was a wad of crumpled dollar bills. "Fourteen dollars," he said. "It isn't much, but it's all I could scrape together without borrowin'. Maybe it'll help him on his journey." He thrust his hand out in a jerky motion. "Here, child, take it. Please take it and give it to Will."

I took it and managed to cram it, like a handful of warm wilted lettuce, in the pocket of my jeans, tucking it carefully into the seamed pocket lining.

When I got home from school, a note from Mama was propped by the sugar bowl. *Dear Sandy, Your Aunt Edie's sick, so I'm over there. Give me a ring. Love, Mama.* I decided to eat a bite first since I was perishing from hunger.

Balancing a submarine sandwich in one hand and the phone in the other, I dialed the number and Mama answered. She gave me a long list of instructions, and between bites I kept saying, "Yes, ma'am." Finally, when I had promised for the umpteenth time to feed the chickens and turkeys, I managed to ask, "What's wrong with Aunt Edie?"

"Sandy, how many times do I have to tell you not to talk with your mouth full of food?" I recognized this for a delaying tactic.

"Yes, Mama." I made a noisy swallow. "Now tell me— what's the matter with Aunt Edie?"

"Nothing to be alarmed about, but she's weak as a dishrag and has had a couple of fainting spells."

"From what?"

"Female trouble," Mama said reluctantly. I gave up. I knew, from years of listening to ladies talk, that female trouble could mean anything from a tilted womb, whatever that is, to cysts the size of grapefruits. I never could figure out why it was always grapefruit—why not croquet balls or oranges? It kills me that I have tubes and ovaries and cycles and all the other dumb things. They haven't all started working in me yet, but with my luck, they will.

"Sandy, you're not listening to me." She was right—I wasn't. It's just as well she repeated the last thing she said. "Today's Wednesday."

"Yes, ma'am," I answered, hoping she couldn't hear me sigh.

"I'll probably be over here for a couple of days, but no matter what I'll be home Friday night to go to Commencement Exercises with you and your father."

"Good, Mama."

Then, as though she was somewhere over in China instead of three miles down the road, Mama said in a homesick voice, "I miss you, baby—take care."

"I will," I answered and then repeated, "I miss you, too." And, sure enough, I did. The kitchen was spotless and empty, like a page in *Family Circle*, and Mama's apron hung limp and lifeless from the hook on the door. Placing a fold of it between my palms, I thought about Mama and how she used to laugh when Wanda and I dressed in her old clothes and spiky high heels, playing grown-up. That was a long time ago. I can barely remember the sound of Mama's laughter. If only the war would get over and Benjie could return home, maybe things would get back to normal.

I sat on the front porch steps and waited for Papa to come home. There wasn't a breath of cool air and the cotton candy pink of the fluffy mimosa blooms drooped in the heat. My tee shirt stuck to the space between my shoulders and little trickles of sweat ran down my legs. I toyed with the idea of going in the house where the fan was stirring an artificial breeze. But I sat there, like a knot on a log, just waiting. I looked down at my sneakers, covered with black-and-white drawings of the Beatles, and I didn't give a rip that John Lennon's face was grass-stained and Ringo Starr was covered with dried mud.

I was relieved to see Papa pull the government car into the driveway. "Hi there, Tom-girl," he called as he was getting out. Then, wiping the back of his neck, he added, "Whew, it's been a scorcher today."

I followed him into the family room where Papa automatically turned on the TV and settled in his recliner.

"I need to talk to you, Papa. It's real important."

"Shoot," he said.

"Well, as you know, Mama's over at Aunt Edie's for the next day or so."

"Yes, she told me she was going. We'll miss her, that's for sure, but don't you think the two of us can manage by ourselves?"

"That's not the problem, Papa." I charged on. "It's just that I'd already promised Wanda I'd spend tomorrow night with her, and I hate to leave you alone in this big old house and all, and if you'd like me to stay with you I'll just tell Wanda—"

"Whoa," Papa said, holding up his hand. "Take it easy, sugar, your motor's racing." He grinned at me. "The goblins won't get me if I spend the night alone. You go ahead with your plans." He glanced at his watch, which showed, straight up and down, six o'clock. Crossing the room to turn on the Channel 4 news, he asked over his shoulder, "You and Wanda planning anything special tomorrow night?"

"We're going frog gigging with Sam and Roy Lee," I

said, the words sticking in my throat. Papa and Mama both put honesty in the same bag with cleanliness and godliness.

The conversation was over. There were other things—a lot of other things—I needed to talk with Papa about, but I knew from experience I couldn't compete with the evening news.

I marched off to the kitchen to set the table for supper, which Mama had prepared in advance and left with a list of instructions thumbtacked to the bulletin board.

> Warm up the butterbeans and okra.
> Slice the ham thin, don't hunk it.
> Peach cobbler is in the Pyrex dish.
> Rinse everything good after supper; don't
> encourage the roaches and sugar ants.

It was almost as though Mama was in the kitchen with me, and I wished she was. A funny thing about mothers —they don't take up much space, but they sure make a hole when they're gone.

When supper was over, Papa pushed his empty plate away and looked across the table at me. "You're being very quiet, Tom-girl. Is anything bothering you?"

"No sir, not really," I said in a low voice. If only I could find the nerve to share my problem of Will hiding out in the tree house. But I couldn't. I'm not much of a gambler, and the risk was too great. As much as I love and trust Papa, I had no way of knowing what he might decide was the right thing to do about Will. I couldn't chance it. Papa might very well feel the proper action to take would be to turn Will over to the sheriff, and I couldn't stand the thought of that.

"Come on, Sandy," Papa urged. "You're upset about

something, and maybe we should talk about it. You can level with me."

I fingered the fringe of my place mat and tried to find the right words, because maybe—just maybe—I could get his opinion on the KKK without involving myself or the Dewberry kids too deeply. They'd torture me to death if I let Papa guess what we were planning to do.

I summoned up all my courage. "Papa, have you heard any talk about a bunch of people here in Hines County who call themselves the Ku Klux Klan?"

Papa looked startled. "Why do you ask?"

"You know how it is—there are rumors at school. All the kids are talking about it lately." That wasn't exactly true, but I had to say something.

"I don't think that's anything to concern yourself about," Papa said firmly.

"But I'd like to know just the same."

Papa replied with obvious reluctance, "Well, I've heard a few rumors myself—especially in the last few months, since all that trouble started up in Alabama and Mississippi with the freedom fighters. But I stay strictly out of it, and my advice to you is to do the same. It's not a topic to meddle with."

"I'm not meddling—I'm simply asking."

"And my advice is still the same: Don't." Papa pushed away from the table. "Is there anything else on your mind?"

"No, sir," I said, trying to sound convincing. There was plenty on my mind—especially now that Papa had practically admitted there was a Ku Klux Klan for real. I had hoped against hope that he would laugh away the whole idea.

"Well, in that case," Papa was saying, "do you want to come watch *Ozzie and Harriet* with me?"

"No, thank you, Papa. I'm going to tidy up, and then I'll get dressed for prayer meeting. Mama or no Mama, it's still Wednesday night."

"How right you are. I'll go shave and find a fresh shirt. Just yell when you're ready, unless you need me to help you tidy up."

I knew Papa was in a gentle way making fun of me but I like the word *tidy*. It's one of those words that sound exactly like it means, *tidy*, nice and neat with no loose ends left dangling. If only I could tidy up some of the mess I'd gotten myself into, I'd sure feel a whole heap better.

CHAPTER 12

Short of roping and hog-tying him, I doubt that you'd ever get Lester O'Kelly inside a church. He didn't look too comfortable even being this close, parked on the side of the road in front of Shiloh Baptist, astride his motorcycle with one foot pawing the ground and Pearl draped all over him.

"Aw come on, Pearl," he was saying, "lemme get gone from here. I'll pick you up at your house when prayer meetin's over."

"Yeah, I bet. You'll get to drinkin' beer and cuttin' the fool with those goons down at the Red Lantern, and you'll forget all about little old me." She giggled. Wanda and I both groaned from where we stood, watching and gagging.

"My drinkin' buddies ain't goons," Lester said. "They's a bunch of good ol' boys."

"Good for nothin'." Pearl gave another giggle.

Lester's hand shot out and gave one of Pearl's boobs a tweak, and Pearl pretended to slap him. "Quit that, Lester, you hear? You'll give me a cancer." The sound she made this time was more a whinny than a giggle.

"Too bad Lester's not a churchgoer," Wanda said in

disgust. "I don't know about speaking in tongues, but he'd be a whiz at laying on hands."

"We don't do that," I reminded her. "That's only the Hard-shell and Primitive Baptists."

"Oh pooh, you're so literal," Wanda said, making it sound like something dirty.

"Well, if you ain't gonna give me any lovin', I'm splittin'," said Lester. He revved his motor and roared off down the road in the direction of the Red Lantern, leaving Pearl like a punctured balloon until she caught sight of a couple of other grown boys puffing hurriedly on last cigarettes before the service started. This pumped her up again and she said something like "Out of sight, out of mind" as she headed their way.

Papa was with a little knot of people off to one side, postponing going inside the church as long as possible. Most of these people had familiar faces and voices, but in the twilight they were strange and scary. Their usual talk of politics and church affairs and the Vietnam War was forgotten as they kicked, back and forth, the subject of the murder and Will and the posse. I edged away from them as old Mr. Barnes was drawling, "Part of a plot, more'n likely. Shoulda packed all them savages back to Africa a hundred years ago."

A hasty check of watches showed eight o'clock and we all trooped inside. Wednesday night prayer meeting is much more relaxed and informal than the Sunday morning worship. Most of the women had on cotton or drip-dry dresses and were hatless, except for Mrs. Dewberry. She had on that frowsy old hat that self-respecting rats wouldn't nest in. There wasn't a tie among the men except for Reverend Parrish's. He probably sleeps and bathes wearing his bow tie and would probably look as naked as a jaybird without it.

94

Papa settled down on the pew with Mr. and Mrs. Dewberry who sat like bookends with May Bell, Sue Nell, and Goober's diaper bag squashed in between them. Goober was dead to the world on Mrs. Dewberry's shoulder.

Wanda gave me a push from the aisle and the hard, unpadded seat spanked my bottom as I plopped down next to Roy Lee. "You don't have to shove," I whispered fiercely to Wanda, who gave me a wicked grin.

Roy Lee shared his hymnal with me, our hands tangling up as we turned to page 58, "Bringing in the Sheaves." Suddenly I wished I was still a little girl, when I just *knew* the people were bringing in the cheese. That was back when I also thought the water in the baptismal pool had to be black and filthy where they washed all those sins away. Roy Lee ducked his head close to mine. "Why the funny smile?"

"I'll tell you later," I said in a low voice, turning my attention to the singing, which was practically drowned out by the asthmatic organ. Miss Cohen was stomping the pedal, her gray beehive of hair bouncing with every beat.

Papa passed the collection plate on our side of the church, and I gave him a wink along with my quarter. Watching him move from pew to pew, I felt a sudden rush of feelings, mixed together like a batter, of love and pride and other good things I couldn't find names for. People have always said I'm truly the spitting image of Papa. I hugged that thought to myself.

The text was read, the sermon begun, and I began to feel uncomfortable. The preacher was sounding off about Vietnam, and I worried about poor Benjie over there fighting, maybe getting wounded or worse, and I knew that lately I hadn't spent nearly enough time worrying and praying for my only brother. And when Reverend

95

Parrish moved back across the ocean to conditions in this country, linking together a lot of big words like *desegregation, retaliation, Nigra militants*, and *a murderer loose in our midst*, I actually squirmed in my seat. I was getting more and more frantic about Will. If that stupid posse had spent the whole day crawling around on all fours, they still would have had more than ample time to search every inch of our swamp. But I knew they hadn't caught Will yet because news like that travels fast, and somebody would have said. Lester would have surely told Pearl, and, furthermore, scattered in the congregation were several men who had been drinking beer at Pinky Pelham's with the posse.

When the preacher turned his sermon over to simpler things like hating and lying and stealing and bearing false witness, I wasn't a bit more comfortable. All I could do was sit there, a miserable sinner, asking the Lord's forgiveness because it was true, I'd had a busy week with my sinning. I had hated the sheriff and his posse, I'd lied to everyone I knew, and I'd stolen food like crazy from Mama's kitchen. I'm not at all sure what bearing false witness means, but I'd probably done some of that, too.

While I was dwelling on my sins, Wanda kept poking me in the ribs and pointing out song titles in the hymnal. I shook my head. I was in enough trouble with the Lord without being sacrilegious. The game she wanted to play was certainly that, if not downright wicked. We've done it for years. Goodness knows where we first came up with the idea. We might have made it up out of sheer Sunday boredom. It's called Between The Sheets. We tack those words to the name of the song, like "Yield Not to Temptation" between the sheets, or "How Great Thou Art" between the sheets. It's a childish game, but when Wanda punched me again, I sighed and gave in. Anything would beat just sitting there stewing myself to death. Besides, maybe the Lord would forgive all my sins in a lump.

"O Happy Day, That Fixed My Choice" between the sheets almost broke us both up, and Wanda and I were holding our breath and making our faces purple trying to stifle our giggles—which is part of the game—when I noticed that Roy Lee was watching us. He's always known exactly the game we were playing, and it never embarrassed me before. But now I could feel the blush spreading up from my scoop-necked blouse to the roots of my shingled hair. I yanked the book from Wanda and closed it firmly, wedging it down by my side under my pleated skirt.

For the rest of the service I stared shamefacedly ahead, Wanda glaring on my right and Roy Lee smiling on the left. In front, Goober was spitting up on his mother's pillowy shoulder. I was weak-kneed with relief when we stood for the closing hymn, the first and last stanza of "Blest Be the Tie That Binds." It was certainly fitting, since Reverend Parrish was tugging away at his spotted bow tie. It was all askew when he begged us to "sing out all together now with feeling."

Even before the last wheezing note of Miss Cohen's organ died away, the preacher pronounced the benediction, mercifully brief, and we all filed outside to fill our lungs with fresh May air.

Mrs. Dewberry, dandling Goober in her arms, was saying to Papa, "Come on, Tom, it's way past this young-un's bedtime but it's still the shank of the evenin'. Why don't you and Sandy stop off and set a spell? I packed down a freezer of banana ice cream before we came to meetin', and it oughta be nice and solid now."

I stood still, waiting for Papa's answer. I'd had enough

of the Dewberry family to last me for a while. But Papa replied without consulting me, "Thanks, Sal—makes my mouth water to think about it. We'd be happy to stop by your house."

Oh well, I thought, with Will on my mind I'd be no better than a gibbering idiot no matter where I went. Besides, Mrs. Dewberry's home-churned ice cream did sound tempting. We're not joking when we call her our neighborhood Dairy Queen.

All but one outside light had been turned off and I saw Miss Cohen stumble a little in a shallow hole. Running over, I helped her find her way to her ancient Cadillac. That car must be a thousand years old, but it goes with her big old house—really a spooky mansion set back in a grove of worn-out pecans, moss covered and no longer bearing. It would scare me skinny to live there all alone.

"Thank you, my dear. It's nice to have a strong young shoulder to lean on." She gave an old lady sigh. "What with one thing and another lately, I'm beginning to feel my age."

"You don't seem old to me," I said, lying again—but maybe white lies don't count against you.

I held open the heavy door and she got behind the wheel, saying almost to herself, "If I had good sense, I'd close up the house and move on down to Miami Beach where I've got some family left."

"Don't do that, Miss Cohen. There's a lot of folks, including me, who would miss you if you left." This time I was telling the truth.

Miss Cohen patted my hand, which was resting on the window frame. "You're a sweet child, Sandy Cason—a very sweet child."

Papa's voice rang out, "You coming, Sandy?"

"Yes, Papa," I called back.

As we drove the short distance to the Dewberry's, I suddenly turned to my father. "Tell me something, Papa—do you think I'm a sweet child?"

Papa didn't blink an eyelid. "Sweeter than honey in a comb." Then more seriously he added, "Yes, Tom-girl, you're sweet—and not only that, you're bright and you're pretty and I love you."

"How much do you love me, Papa," I asked. What if he had forgotten?

"I love you like heck—more than a speck—a bushel and a peck and a hug around the neck," he said in the old familiar singsong, and I relaxed.

While we all looked for places on the Dewberry porch, Mrs. Dewberry handed Goober over to Pearl. "Go change his didy and poke him in his crib."

"Why me?" Pearl whined. "I'm waiting for Lester."

"Pester Lester. Go on, do as I tell you. Lester'll keep," was Mrs. Dewberry's calm reply, placing the soppy baby in Pearl's reluctant arms. Still grumbling and holding Goober away from her as though he were a sack of rotten potatoes, Pearl stomped into the house, kicking the screen door *bang* behind her.

Mrs. Dewberry turned to Wanda and issued another order. "Now, you, go fetch the bowls and the spoons."

"Make Roy Lee—he isn't doing anything," said Wanda, sounding just like Pearl.

"None of your sass, Miss Priss—scat." Mrs. Dewberry turned to the rest of us. "Law me, if ever one time those younguns would do as they're told, I vow I'd faint and fall in it." She started removing the wet croaker sacks from the top of the mammoth ice-cream churn, and the twins crowded close, all over each other.

May Bell said, "It's my turn to lick the dasher."

Sue Nell gave her sister a shove. "Ain't neither. You had it last time."

Carefully easing the dasher out, Mrs. Dewberry said, "Quiet, you two. You can lick it together."

"Germs! I don't want her dirty old germs," they shrieked in one voice.

"Suit yourself," said Mrs. Dewberry, not the least bit ruffled. "We'll give it to Sandy. Anyway, she's company."

The Gruesome Twosome made monstrous faces at me when Mrs. Dewberry handed it over. I ignored them and started licking, the ice cream cold and soothing to the swollen gum around the twelve-year molar I was cutting.

In the middle of second helpings, Lester rode up on his motorcycle. And seated behind him, of all people, was Mr. Wall-Eye Weaver, a mismatched pair if there ever was one.

Mr. Wall-Eye lives down the road, and his real name is Wallace Weaver, but everybody calls him Wall-Eye. If ever a man fit his name, he does. He's skinny as a piece of string, and he's got large staring eyes with practically no iris, which makes him look exactly like a walleyed perch. His Adam's apple is huge, like a goiter, and bobs up and down every time he swallows. It was doing that now as he said, "Howdy."

They both refused ice cream, which is just as well—I've heard that beer and ice cream can give you ptomaine poisoning. Or is it watermelon and beer? At any rate, from the way they were weaving up the walk, they didn't need anything else.

Off to one side, Pearl was hissing at Lester, "Why on earth have you got that dumb old coot with you?"

Lester smoothed down one of his sideburns. "Danged if I know. He was on foot and headed in this direction."

"Man, what a wearisome day," Mr. Wall-Eye said from where he sat, propped against a pillar to the porch. "Tryin' to keep up with them bloodhounds of Sheriff Wiggins can tucker a fellow plumb out."

"You never said a truer word," Lester agreed. "It'll cold separate the men from the boys."

"Did you pick up a trail?" asked Papa, setting his empty ice cream plate to one side.

Mr. Wall-Eye answered, "Pshaw, we ain't picked up nothin' but seed ticks and chiggers—to say nothin' of a million mosquito bites." He clawed at his ankle, remembering. "For one thing, them dogs acted plumb loco, goin' round and round in circles, and headin' right back to Hines City. Away from the swamp altogether." He scratched again. "I got no faith in them dogs. They're crazy as bedbugs."

I carefully let out my held-in breath.

Lester, still standing in the yard at the edge of the steps, spoke up. "From what the sheriff said, we gonna try the swamps again tomorrow at first daylight. That nigger's gotta be hidin' back in those swamps. Ain't nowhere else he could be."

I was sitting on the bottom step, close enough to kick old Lester, and believe me, I felt like doing just that. Instead, I looked down at Roy Lee's hands—he was sitting beside me—making a cat's cradle out of string. In the dim light from the naked bulb at the end of the porch, his fingers looked thin and spidery.

Mr. Dewberry was saying in his rusty voice, "It's a puzzle to me how that boy could've disappeared from the face of the globe without leavin' some kind of trace."

101

Mr. Wall-Eye bobbed his Adam's apple. "It's peculiar, sure 'nough. The only answer I can come up with is that he finagled some sucker into helpin' him."

I sat motionless, staring at the moths hurling themselves to death against the heated bulb.

Lester stretched and gave himself a Tarzan thump on his tee-shirted chest. "Come on, Pearl, I'm rarin' to go— we need to get back and close up the old Red Lantern."

"Sure, Lester," Pearl said. "Just give me a minute to go do my face."

Wanda, who had been fairly quiet until now, piped up from the swing, "I think what you ought to do with that face is trade it in for one that's human."

"And I don't give a doodly-squat what you think," said Pearl as she hightailed it through the screen door with another *bang*.

The moon was full. With it and the light from the porch I could see Lester real plain—his slick sideburns, his flat gray eyes the color of freshwater clams, the thin-lipped mouth, puckered now as he whistled air through his teeth and sneered in Wanda's direction. His feet in the shiny boots were toed out, and he stood with the lower part of his body jutting out like a cheap imitation of Elvis Presley.

Suddenly, near the toe of Lester's boot, I caught sight of a little baby chicken, round and fluffy as a dandelion puff, its yellow down grayed by the moonlight. Poor little biddy, lost from its nest and its mother. Leaning way over, I held out my hand and barely whispered, "Here, baby, come over here. I'll put you back in the nest." It was moving in my direction when without warning, Lester O'Kelly's boot lifted up, not high, and came down quick and heavy, pressing hard on top of the tiny chicken.

For a second, I sat there sickened and stunned. Lester lifted his foot and turned to Mrs. Dewberry. "Ma'am, I'm awful afraid I stepped on one of your little biddies, purely an accident. Sure didn't mean to do it."

Hearing that, I sprang to my feet as though jerked by invisible wires. Without thinking or planning, I hurled myself headlong at Lester, pushing with both my hands, and knocked him out of the way. Kneeling down, I picked up the lifeless chicken, as silent and weightless as balled-up dust. I held it gently, still warm in my hand, as I screamed at Lester O'Kelly, "You did it on purpose! I saw you do it on purpose! You're mean and ugly and cruel."

It may never be really clear to me what happened next. I could feel myself letting go. The fear and suspense and confusion of the last awful days swirled around like a whirlpool, sucking me under. I have only a dim recollection of everyone staring at me as though I had turned into a raving lunatic and little tags of sentences were swarming around my head: "had to be accidental," "She's just hysterical," "Nobody else saw Lester do anything," and, worse than that, "You know how girls can get at a certain time."

I became aware that Papa, strong and steady, was holding me close and letting me cry all over his shirtfront, and Roy Lee was timidly patting me on the shoulder. They had no way of knowing that only a part of those tears were for the poor little chicken. Another part was for Will and all his problems. And another part for me. I still had that whirlpool feeling, and nobody likes to drown.

CHAPTER 13

The next night at supper, Papa looked disgusted at the tuna casserole, and I couldn't blame him. It's a mystery to me how it burned on the edges and still stayed frozen in the middle. Mama's empty place seemed to take up most of the table, and both of us were glad to escape to the family room when we cleared the plates away.

Standing by Papa's recliner, I cleared my throat. "Papa, are you sure you don't want me to stay here with you tonight? There's nothing that says I have to spend the night with Wanda."

"You go right ahead with your plans, Tom-girl," Papa replied. "Do you want me to drive you over?"

"No, thank you, Papa. It's still full daylight and I'd like to walk." Of course, what I'd rather have done was run, not walk, in the other direction, landing up anywhere besides the Dewberry house.

Papa was deep in the six o'clock news when I kissed him good-bye. I hugged him so hard that he looked up, surprised. "Take it easy, honey—this isn't farewell forever. I'll see you tomorrow."

"I know," I said and grabbed my little wad of overnight clothes and ran.

The setting sun cast huge, blurry shadows around me. My own shape moved and stretched like gray Silly Putty with every step, adding to my unreal feeling. I went over in my mind how things used to be in Hines County, peaceful and boring, with nothing ever happening. Just a short time ago, it was front page news if anyone broke a leg; and the biggest excitement in years was when the Methodist preacher's daughter eloped with the tightrope walker from the Ringling Brothers Circus. How could things change in such a hurry? It's no wonder I was flat-out not believing the things that were happening now, starting with last week's murder. Even the word seemed strange and foreign to Hines City. And I was not believing that, at that very moment, there was a posse out there somewhere searching for a hometown boy. Then *this*—I truly could not believe I was on my way to spy on the Ku Klux Klan.

As I neared the Dewberry house, I decided two things: Hard as it is to imagine, there might be a Klan, but nobody in his right mind would belong to it, and, certainly, nobody in his right mind would risk being caught spying on their meeting. And that included me. Sam and Wanda and Roy Lee could go and get themselves lynched if they wanted to, but I wasn't about to set foot in Willetts' pasture. Deciding that, I breathed a little easier and felt almost relaxed as I walked up on the Dewberry porch.

As usual after supper, the porch was overflowing with Dewberrys of every age and size, all of them talking at once, so it sounded like a Holy Roller meeting. Even that hateful Lester O'Kelly was there to add to the confusion, but he was on his way out. He was saying something to Pearl about leaving to shoot some pool with the boys and her lip was poking out a mile.

I found myself wedged in the swing between Wanda

and Roy Lee like the filling in a sandwich, trying to make myself as small as possible. Mrs. Dewberry finally raised her voice above the rest and spoke directly to me. "Sandy, how's your Aunt Edie doin'? I been meanin' to get over there and see her. But what with cannin' peaches and field peas and tryin' to keep all these hungry mouths fed, I don't get a moment to call my own." Scarcely pausing to take a breath, she went on, "It's a cryin' shame about her losin' the baby; but like I told Ernest, I figger the good Lord knows what He's doin'. After all, He giveth and He taketh away."

I felt like I'd been hit in the stomach. So that's what's been the matter with Aunt Edie, and all of them letting me think it was plain old female trouble—something simple that Geritol and Lydia E. Pinkham would soon fix up. Grown-ups really don't play fair at times. Maybe I could have figured it out for myself if Aunt Edie wasn't so blasted fat.

Mrs. Dewberry wasn't even aware she'd given me a shock and was talking on a mile a minute. "Sometimes I almost wish He'd seen fit not to let me bear so many children, but I'm not complainin'. Now that I've got them, I wouldn't part with a single one of them, even if they do worry the livin' life out of me most of the time." Shifting Goober in her lap, she gave his shoulder a loving pat. "No, I take that back—I pride myself on the fact that I don't worry too much. Take this matter of lettin' you kids go frog giggin' tonight. There's a lot of people that'd say I ain't got no business lettin' kids your age go down to the pond at night, but I don't reckon there's any harm in it, if you don't get in that boggy place where that man sank down over his head. That poor man—he's still buried in that quicksand. Even with grapplin' hooks they never did find his body. They looked and looked."

I had heard that story so many times I quit listening. Besides, it all happened ages ago, during World War II. Leaning over, I whispered in Wanda's ear, "I might as well tell you, I've changed my mind. I'm not going."

She grabbed my arm and spluttered, "What do you mean, you're not going?"

"Just what I said. I'm not going with you. You can like it or lump it."

Wanda reached behind me and tugged at Roy Lee's shirt. "Talk some sense to Scaredy Cat here. She says she's not going."

Before Roy Lee had a chance to reply, Sam stuck his head out the front screen door and motioned to us. "Come on, gang, it's time to head for the pond. I can hear them bullfrogs callin', so let's get our gear together."

I rose from the swing and went around to the back of the house with the others. I couldn't just take off and go back home without some kind of explanation. While Roy Lee and Sam rummaged around in the plunder house for nets and baskets and gigging spears to convince their folks we were really after frogs, Wanda whirled on me. "Now tell me loud and clear just why you aren't going."

Stubbornly, I stood my ground. "I decided it's a dumb idea, and besides it's dangerous."

Wanda stuck her hands on her hips and glared at me. "Well, if that isn't something! So now you want to ruin it for everybody else." She turned to Roy Lee. "Can you do anything with her?"

"I doubt it," Roy Lee said. "What do you want me to do, hog-tie her and drag her along?"

Wanda shot back, "Seriously, can't you persuade her to change her mind?"

"Wanda, Sandy might be the only one with sense. This could be dangerous," Roy Lee said, reaching out to lay his hand on my arm. "I tell you what," he said to me, "if anything looks like it might go wrong, I'll bring you back to the house. OK?"

Finally, I shrugged my shoulders and managed to mumble, "OK."

Then the four of us, loaded down with all the gigging stuff, trudged around to the front of the house to say good-bye.

"You all be careful, you hear me?" Mrs. Dewberry said. "And watch out for snakes, especially the water moccasins. That pond is purely loaded with them."

As we turned to leave, Pearl stopped us all in our tracks. "Now that Lester's gone to horse around with his buddies, I think I'll go with you. Anything beats staying here bored out of my cotton-pickin' mind."

There we stood like dummies until Mrs. Dewberry solved the problem for us. "Pearl, sugar, ain't you forgettin'? *Peyton Place* is on TV tonight."

Pearl gave a little snap of her fingers. "Holy cow, you're right. I sure wouldn't want to miss that."

We left hurriedly, before Pearl had a chance to change her mind again. When we reached the very last of the junked cars in the worn-out field, Roy Lee pried open the rusty trunk and we stashed the gigging gear inside, keeping only the flashlight. Then, single file, we struck off down the path that leads to the old dirt road which goes by the sawdust pile. That shortcut made it much closer to the Willett place, but it was spookier than going by the paved main road.

Now we were walking in twos and I stuck close to Roy Lee. The moon was coming up, fat and full, and I wished for a cloud to hide it. All this light made the walking easier, but I'd sure have felt safer if we'd had a cover of darkness.

In a low voice, Roy Lee asked, "Sandy, you still scared?"

"Spitless," I said. And I was. I would have given my next ten years' allowance to be safely home in bed with my pillow over my head.

"Try not to worry about it. I think all that's going to come of this is a good long walk."

"But what about Sam's information? Is he making all this up?"

"You know Sam's never got anything straight in his life. On the other hand, I don't think he's got enough imagination to make up a story like this, so more than likely somebody's pulling his leg, and it's all just some kind of joke."

"Let's hope," I said, suddenly jumping away from a fallen twig that looked like a snake in the sandy rut.

Roy Lee laughed. "You're nervous as a cat in a roomful of rocking chairs."

In silence we walked on, Wanda and Sam ahead of us setting the pace. In spite of Wanda's bluff, she walked with a crouching motion up against Sam's shoulder. She was nowhere near as brave as she pretended.

Finally, when I had all but given up, we reached the Willett property, climbed a split-rail fence, and sat down under an oak tree in one corner. That way we had a clear view of the open pasture and yet weren't near enough to be seen if the Ku Klux Klan actually showed up. I'm not sure even Sam believed they would, but the possibility was enough to make my blood run cold.

I was sitting in an ant pile and I could feel them crawling all over my feet and ankles, so I moved over a few feet. Sam hissed at me, "Stay still, Fidgety. Makin' all this commotion. We should've left you home."

I could tell by the tone of Sam's voice that he was

109

nervous too, so I ignored him. I just sat there staring out at the pasture, wishing that if the Klan was planning to come, they'd come and get it over with. Every now and then I'd see some lightning bugs and think it was the Klansmen coming, but it wasn't. I tried to kill time by saying the alphabet from Z to A. And when that didn't work, I practiced the Gettysburg Address; but the words were plain old gibberish, so I quit with that.

"Let's go," I whispered but got no answer from any of them.

A few more minutes crawled by and I begged again, "*Please*, let's go."

This time Roy Lee backed me up. "Suits me—I'm more than ready."

It was Sam who replied in a low, husky voice, "Dry up, you two—we ain't budgin' from here."

So we continued to sit, not talking, not doing anything but feeling miserable and uncomfortable, for what was beginning to seem like forever. Even Sam was shifting around, I hoped ready to give up and head back home, when suddenly we saw a light approaching from the far side of the pasture. It kept coming closer and closer, growing bigger and bigger, and I wanted to close my eyes but I couldn't.

I stared at the light. It was near enough now to take on the shape of a large fiery cross which was being carried along by four or five figures in long white robes with white masks over their heads. Only the top of the tall wooden cross was burning, shedding light on the other figures that moved along in a huddle. There must have been two or three dozen of them, and it looked for an awful moment like they were walking straight toward us. Then they stopped and stuck the burning cross in the ground. It lit up the whole sky and made a huge puddle of light around them. They were close enough now that I could make out their feet sticking out from beneath their robes—ordinary feet with ordinary men's shoes on, loafers and sneakers and oxfords and boots. I fastened my mind on those shoes, trying not to see the white-robed, unreal figures. But in spite of myself, I looked. The Klansmen were moving in circles around the cross, and we could hear them chanting something that sounded like long Bible verses.

The four of us squeezed together as close as we could against the trunk of the tree, trying not to breathe. Roy Lee had reached for my hand and was holding it so tight my fingers felt numb. Wanda had clamped her hand across her mouth and was staring, bug-eyed, at the burning cross. And Sam, slack-jawed and stupid-looking, never took his eyes away from the moving figures. I was paralyzed, frozen stiff, and I wished the earth would open up and swallow us all. Anything would be better than having the Klansmen catch us.

The chanting had stopped, and now the men appeared to be listening to one of their leaders who had perched himself on a stump with the other men crowded around him. The leader looked bigger than life, an oversized puppet, as he waved his arms in the flickering light from the cross. I was filled with terror each time he lifted his flowing sleeves and the men roared back their response to whatever he was saying. I tried to pretend I was watching *Birth of a Nation* on the late show or purposely scaring myself in the Hall of Horrors at the Halloween carnival—but I couldn't pretend. This was happening, taking place *now*, in Willetts' pasture, and I was scared out of my wits.

The leader got down from his stump and joined the other men who were making loud noises, some of them yelling, as they marched round and round the still burning cross. Then they stopped, dead still, while four or five men, like grown-up altar boys, lit torches from the fire to guide their way across the pasture. But when they started to leave, instead of going back the way they came, the whole procession moved across in our direction. We stopped breathing. Then they turned sort of catercorner and went off across the field at the far corner. I gulped for air.

Sam whispered, "C'mon, let's follow them. They must not be going far if they're gonna walk, and I want to see what they're up to."

Wanda and I said together, "You're crazy, Sam." And Roy Lee added, "I agree. I think we ought to go home."

"You're all a bunch of yellow-bellied sissies," Sam sneered. "Ain't nothin' gonna happen to us if we keep our distance."

I'll never know why we let Sam lead us away from the oak tree, but suddenly we were following after the Klansmen. We walked carefully and our sneakered feet didn't make much noise. Once in a while one of us would stumble in a gopher hole or on a root, but the moon was shining even brighter now and we could see pretty well. The Klansmen were well ahead of us, the torches bobbing and weaving through the darkness. Some of the men seemed to be carrying another, unlighted cross which slowed their progress a little. It was easy to keep them in sight, although we kept as much distance as possible, with all of us hugging the shadows at the edge of the woods. We were following an old logging trail—or maybe it's a firebreak—which was cleared out fairly well, but the trees were thick on both sides.

Way up ahead, the Klansmen had stopped at a bend in the trail in front of a little house. I didn't even know there was a house out in this part of the woods, but then I guess I'd never been down this far on the Willetts' property.

We stopped under the biggest tree with the darkest shadow we could find, and strained to see what was going on. Everything was quiet. The Klansmen were planting the other big cross in the ground and setting fire to it with their torches. It must have been pure pitch pine because in no time at all it was burning as bright as the one they had left back there in the pasture.

Somebody yelled from inside the house, and then the men in the robes started talking real loud and yelling back at the house. We had no way of knowing if the Klan had planned in advance to do what happened next or if they were acting on impulse, but two of the Klansmen took torches they were carrying and set fire to the tiny shack—that's really all it was, not a house at all—and when it started burning real good, a young black man and a woman with a baby in her arms came running out. They must have been in bed because the woman had on a nightgown and the man didn't have a shirt on, just a pair of pants, and they were barefoot.

Then two or three men grabbed hold of the black man and motioned to another of the sheeted figures who was cracking a big horsewhip through the air and shouting, "Let me at him." He followed this with a braying laugh I recognized at once. It was Lester O'Kelly.

"On, no," I cried, clutching at Roy Lee's shirt, "that crazy goon will kill him."

Seizing my clenched-up hands, Roy Lee forced them still. "Easy, Sandy, easy," he whispered. His grip was hurting me and I struggled to pull loose.

I made myself look again. The scene was clear and vivid in the red orange light of the fire, but it was hard to sort out what was going on. The Klansmen seemed to be arguing among themselves. Several of the men in robes were tugging at Lester, trying to take the whip away, but Lester kept whipping it through the air and laughing that awful laughter. Then the men who had been doing the arguing stalked off across the pasture and the nightmare grew worse. One of the men was dragging a little, with a limp like Mr. Dewberry's, although I told myself it couldn't, just simply *couldn't* be.

When Lester drew back the whip to strike the black man on the ground, I whirled away and started running for home. Blinded by tears, I kept tangling with blackberry briars and stumbling over roots. But I kept running and I couldn't stop crying. Roy Lee was close up behind me, but I didn't slow down. My breath was coming hard and hurting, which made me sick at my stomach. I was forced to stop. Leaning my head against the rough bark of a pine tree, I was plenty sick. Roy Lee, thank goodness, had enough sense to stay away from me until I was through.

I shuddered with one last heave and mopped at my eyes with the back of my hand. Moving closer, Roy Lee said, "Maybe you'll feel better now."

"Well, I don't," I barked at him. "I feel awful." I don't know why I was yelling at Roy Lee. None of this was his fault, but I had to storm at somebody.

We were taking a different route, which came out at State 27, with my house off in one direction and the Dewberry house in the other. Wanda and Sam were running for home without a backward glance. Roy Lee blocked my path by stepping in front of me.

"Sandy, what are you going to do?"

"I'm going home and get Papa—"

"And what will you tell your father?"

"The truth. I'm sure he'll go back there and see about that family." I started running again, as fast as I could, with Roy Lee pounding beside me step by step until we reached my house. He was still right with me when I jerked the screen door open and raced to the family room.

Papa must have dozed off in his recliner, but now he sprang to his feet, his eyes wide with alarm, when we burst into the room. "What in the name of God—?"

"Papa, it's awful—you've got to go to Willetts' pasture— They're down there now—they're killing those people. Hurry, Papa, hurry—" My words were tripping up in sobs, and I was shaking Papa's arm.

Papa gathered me up and was holding me close against him firmly, saying over my head to Roy Lee, "Son, tell me what's going on. What's the meaning of this?"

Roy Lee braced himself. "It's like Sandy said, Mr. Cason. The Ku Klux Klan held a meeting in Willetts' pasture, and they set fire to a little shack that belongs to a family of blacks."

Papa held me off at arm's length and questioned me with his eyes, saying, "Have a seat, you two. Let's get to the bottom of this mess."

Frantically, I clutched at his sleeve and found my voice again. "But, Papa, there isn't any time to talk. You've got to go stop them!"

"I'm not going anywhere until you've explained," Papa said stubbornly, practically pushing me and Roy Lee down on the couch. "Now, start at the beginning."

He kept picking away at both of us until he had the full story. When we ran out of words, Papa shook his head and said slowly, "This beats all I've ever heard."

I tried again. "Papa, *please* go see if you can do anything. You know how crazy Lester O'Kelly is. He might beat those people to death—even the little baby."

"Roy Lee," Papa interrupted, "did you kids actually see Lester using a whip?"

"Well, no sir, not exactly," Roy Lee said. "We were running in the other direction—but I think Sandy's right. I think they were fixing to—"

"Papa, *please*," I said.

"No, Sandy, I'm not going. Whatever is going on in Willetts' pasture is none of my business."

I couldn't believe my ears. Jumping to my feet again, I sprang at Papa. "But you've got to go! You can't just stand here, doing nothing. You've got to go!"

"No," Papa said with equal determination. "I'm sure it's all over now. The best thing to do is forget it."

I caught sight of myself in the mantel mirror—a grimy, tear-streaked, rumpled stranger. And I sounded like a stranger. "If you don't go, Papa, I'll never in a million years forgive you."

Papa gave me a hard, cold look across the space between us. "I'm going to my room," he said. "We'll settle this in the morning. You've got some explaining to do, young lady, and it better be good." Then, ignoring me completely, he turned to Roy Lee. "Thank you for seeing her home. Do you want me to drive you back to your house?"

"No sir," Roy Lee said. "I don't mind walking. I'll be leaving in just a little while."

"That might be best," said Papa. "It's getting pretty late." Without his usual good-night kiss or one single word to me, Papa went to his bedroom. His door closed with a dull, heavy *thunk*.

Slumping down in the couch, I looked over at Roy Lee. He had pushed his baseball cap to the back of his head and propped his chin in his folded hands, staring off into

116

space. I got to my feet. "Let's go in the kitchen. I'll get us something to drink."

Still not a word from Roy Lee as I opened two 7-Ups and set them on the kitchen table. We sat there making rings on the Formica top, barely looking at each other. Finally, taking a swallow, I said, "I'm not believing this about Papa. I just knew for sure he'd rush down there to help those people out."

"Maybe you shouldn't blame him, Sandy. What could he have done?"

"I don't know," I admitted miserably, "but he could have tried to do something."

"Well, at least he wasn't there at the beginning, like my father was."

So it hadn't been my imagination. That *had* been Mr. Dewberry meeting with the Klan. The only thing I could come up with was, "Perhaps we were mistaken—it was awful dark."

"It wasn't that dark—not with a full moon, a burning cross, and a house on fire." He tugged at the bill of his cap. "I've known for a long time now that Pa was up to something. He couldn't have been going to that many meetings of Elks and Masons, even throwing in the VFW."

I tried to comfort him. "Well, at least he didn't take part in the worst of it. He left when they started to beat that man."

"Yeah, I know." He lapsed into silence again and the steady tick of the kitchen clock was the only sound in the room.

I took a deep breath and slowly let it out again. "Roy Lee, what are you thinking about?"

"I don't know—this whole night's been like some

117

weird dream. I feel like I'm walking around in my sleep."

"Me, too," I admitted. For a good five minutes or so, we kept on sitting there, thinking our own private thoughts, hunched up and miserable. When at last I spoke, my voice sounded loud in the quiet kitchen. I toned it down to little more than a whisper. "Why would those awful Klansmen want to burn down somebody's house?"

"Beats me. I guess because a black family lived in it."

"That's no reason and you know it."

"Yeah, I know it and you know it, but maybe it was reason enough for the Ku Klux Klan."

"But why?" I persisted.

"Lord, Sandy, I don't know. A lot of whites are all stirred up against the blacks right now—with the civil rights thing and stuff like that. Or maybe because the sheriff and the posse still haven't caught Will Brown. So far he's plain outsmarted them and that's bound to sting a little."

This unexpected mention of Will almost threw me into a panic. I held myself rigid as Roy Lee finished his drink and kept on talking. "I'd sure like to know what's happened to Will. I'm hoping he got across the border to Florida. I never did think for a minute he murdered that stupid woman."

My heart was pounding and my nails were digging into the palms of my clenched-up hands. I was aching—really aching—to spill out everything to Roy Lee, but I couldn't. I simply couldn't. Not yet. I deliberately changed the subject. "Well, tell me something else, Roy Lee. Who do you think those men are? People from Hines City? People we might know?"

"We know at least two of them—my father and Lester

O'Kelly," Roy Lee said in a voice that was brittle and cracking a little.

There was nothing to say to that.

Adjusting his cap on his tousled head, Roy Lee pushed away from the table and we both stood up. Silently we walked to the front of the house and he stepped out on the porch. With our noses close to the mesh of the dark screen door, we whispered good-bye.

Papa was standing, arms folded, at the door of his bedroom, and the look on his face was stern and unloving. Timidly, I said in a small, low voice, "Good night, Papa."

Very politely and coldly, Papa replied, "Good night, Cassandra."

My eyes were brimming with tears as I made my way down the hall to my room. Before they could start spilling over, I dashed them away with cold water as I washed my face for bed.

Shivering, I curled up in a tight round ball and pulled the cover over my head, feeling like a scared little kid. I chewed painfully on my knuckles and tried to regulate my breathing, waiting for sleep to come. Finally, it did.

CHAPTER 14

Daylight was streaming in when I opened my eyes the next morning. I hurriedly got out of bed, dressed, and walked to the kitchen. Papa was at the table, measuring instant coffee with a spoon. "Good morning," he said as he poured the boiling water in his cup. Reaching behind him, he placed the kettle back on the stove.

"Good morning," I mumbled, dumping some Cheerios in a cereal bowl and pouring on milk. I sat across from Papa, poking the round little Os, watching them grow swollen and soggy, drinking up all the milk.

Anything would be better than all this silence, so I cleared my throat and blurted out, "Why didn't you want to go help those people last night? I just knew you'd go. I was counting on you to help them."

Papa leaned back in his chair and gave me a long hard look. "Apparently, Sandy, you've heard that the best line of defense is attack. But it won't work with me. Before we start a question and answer session, let's hear from you. What the hell were you kids doing in Willetts' pasture?"

I tried not to squirm. "Do we have to talk about that right now?"

"We have to talk about it some time—why not now? So far I haven't come up with a suitable punishment. Not only did you lie to me, what you did was foolish, even dangerous. You could have been—" He didn't finish the sentence. He just sat there shaking his head.

"Papa, I know—and I'm sorry." There was no way to put into words *how* sorry. "But us being there has nothing to do with what those terrible men did. It was so cruel and awful—the worst thing I've ever seen in my life—" I shuddered, remembering, and my voice dropped lower. "I can't believe you wouldn't want to help those people. Wouldn't you have rushed down there if they'd been white?"

Papa rubbed at his red-rimmed eyes. He must have had trouble sleeping, too. "Maybe we better talk about this some other time. It's Memorial Day and I don't have a mail delivery, but your bus will be along most any minute."

I looked up at the clock. "Papa, there's lots of time left. Please answer my questions."

Papa sighed and ran his hand through his disheveled hair. "OK, Sandy—fire away."

He looked awfully tired but I hardened my heart against him. I couldn't just let the whole matter drop. "Did you not want to go because they were black?"

"That had nothing to do with it," Papa snapped. "I simply felt that whatever was going on was none of my business."

"But it's always been your business before to try to help people when they're in trouble." I spooned the clinging Cheerios from the side of the bowl, squishing them in the center.

"In other words, Sandy, you think I let you down by not dashing out of here on some wild goose chase?"

"But it wasn't a wild goose chase. Roy Lee and I were telling you the truth. The Ku Klux Klan was there and

121

they beat that man, maybe killed him, and they were hurting that woman—"

"All right, so you were telling the truth. What did you think I could do, single-handed? You might prefer to think so, but I'm not Superman."

There was no answer to that. He was right. One man alone, even Papa, couldn't stand up by himself against a whole bunch of lunatics. But he could have tried. He could have wanted to. Yes, I felt let down.

Papa was saying, "I'm your father, Sandy, and I don't have to justify any behavior on my part. Do you understand that?"

"Yes, sir," I said, shrinking a little. That argument from him or Mama always defeats me.

But Papa was justifying a little when he added, "There really wasn't anything I could do about last night, and I'm sorry. I'm sorry the whole thing happened. Violence certainly isn't the answer to the problems facing us. It can only make bad matters worse."

I glanced at the clock again. We still had a little bit of time and I wanted to keep Papa talking. I've always believed in miracles; maybe one now would make it possible for me to tell Papa about Will. I'd reached a point where I simply had to have his help. There was nobody else to turn to. "Tell me Papa, why do you think the Klan would do a thing like that?"

"*Why*? I don't really know. You take a bunch of rednecks like that and they're running scared. All their lives, the only thing they've had going for them is the fact they're white. For some that's enough in itself, but for others, it isn't that simple. They really believe the black race is inferior and has to be kept in line no matter what, and that the best way to keep them subjected is through fear and intimidation."

Some of what Papa was saying was way over my head. I tried to get him to reduce it down. Besides, this wasn't the way to lead up to my problem with Will. I tried again. "How do you personally feel?"

"About what?"

"About blacks. I really need to know. Do you like them?"

Papa pulled at his earlobe, thinking, and then he said, "I no longer know how I feel. I guess my answer would have to be no, not really. I like a few of them, respect a lot of them, would never deliberately hurt a one of them, and yet, as for liking the race as a whole—no."

"But why?"

"I don't know exactly. I guess it all goes back to the way I was taught to think when I was growing up. And, to be more specific, although I don't consider myself a white supremacist or part of some master race, there are times I look around me—when I see a bunch of sorry no-account Negroes whooping it up on Saturday night—and I realize there's nothing on God's green earth that will ever convince me they're my equal."

"But Papa," I exploded, "that isn't fair—judging people by the color of their skin. Besides, what's color got to do with anything? What happens to *all men are created equal*? And what about those loudmouthed drunks at Fannie's Red Lantern? Are they your equals just because they're white?"

Papa held up his hand. "Wait just a minute, Sandy—let me finish now that we've started this. I'm not apologetic about my feelings about blacks—my attitude towards the black race doesn't necessarily make me inhuman or a hating person. What I am is a Southerner with my roots in a divided South—and dividing it up into black and white started way before my time."

"But Papa, this is *my* time now. Things are different, not like they used to be when you were growing up."

Sloshing his stone cold coffee around in his cup, Papa said slowly, "I admit, Sandy, it's very complicated. Maybe when you get a little older you'll understand it better."

"I doubt *that*," I replied, giving my forehead a smack with the heel of my palm. "It's just the opposite—the older I get, the more mixed up I am. I don't want to wish my life away, but sometimes I'd like to close my eyes and wake up grown."

"If you want my opinion, Tom-girl, I think you're rushing things. Why don't you relax and not bother yourself with all this business of white versus black? Things will work out, you'll see."

"But it isn't just white and black." I fumbled for words. "It's things like fair and unfair, right and wrong, trusting and not trusting—" I waved my hands with a helpless feeling. "What am I supposed to do with all those things you've hammered into my head for twelve long years— wad them up and throw them away like used up Kleenex?"

What I wanted to say and couldn't was: What do I do for a daddy I can turn to now that I really need him? There Papa was, sitting close enough to touch, but he might as well have been the man in the moon, with a billion miles between us.

My face must have shown how truly baffled I felt, because Papa's tone was soft and concerned. "I'm sorry, baby, if the answers I've given you are not the answers you want. But you asked, and I tried to answer with the truth as I see it."

In the silence that followed, I could hear Mr. Tate

honking the school bus horn—the first time all year I hadn't been outside waiting. With a hasty good-bye to Papa, I streaked down the hall and out of the house, letting the front screen door slam behind me.

For some reason, Miss Everett looked as miserable as I felt. Her face was pale and pinched-up as she called the class to order in a low, tired voice. She made a few brief announcements, telling us things we already knew: This last day of school would be over at noon; Commencement Exercises would be held in the school auditorium at eight o'clock, and those on the program were to be there promptly at seven thirty, without fail; and there would be one last rehearsal right after midmorning recess.

Time crept by in quiet confusion. Two or three kids left the room to return some overdue books to the library and three or four others left with trumped-up excuses. All around me, my classmates were fidgeting, squirming around in their seats, doing dumb things like erasing penciled notes from the margins of textbooks or throwing spitballs like a bunch of second graders. I just sat, motionless, folded into myself. My thoughts were like tangled twine, hopelessly snarled, and in my mind a warped old record kept repeating, over and over, *Why, Papa, why?* Trusting Papa completely had been the most important thing in my life. I could always count on Papa to be fair and wise and full of understanding. To question him now turned my whole world topsy-turvy.

Hunched up as I was, one part of me kept watching Miss Everett, pacing, pacing, back and forth in front of the room. She kept slapping the paint stirrer against her palm. Then she stopped in front of her desk and spoke to us. "I've debated in my mind what I'm going to say to you—I've even debated whether or not I should say any-thing at all. I've decided, right or wrong, that I simply can't stay quiet—I would never forgive myself."

There wasn't a sound in the room as we all sat listen-ing, really listening, to Miss Everett. "It has been a long year—a very long year—and an awful lot has happened all over the world. We've talked about a lot of these things in class. All of us held our breath back in March with the Gemini III flight. Accomplishments like that are really marvelous, in every sense of the word. Giant strides are being made in the exploration of outer space, and I truly believe that small steps are being taken toward world peace and a better relationship between Christians and non-Christians. These things are good, totally worthwhile, but"—she helplessly shrugged her shoul-ders then squared them up again—"most of the last year has also been a season of tragedy, with riots in California and New York, all over the place. There have been racial disturbances and looting and brutal beatings, even kill-ings. Especially here in the South." Now she was pacing again but continued to talk. "Like a bunch of ostriches, we kept hoping we wouldn't be touched by what was going on in Alabama and Mississippi. As long as the freedom riders and the demonstrators and the Ku Klux Klan didn't come across our borders, we'd be safe here in Georgia. We wouldn't be a part of the brutality and hatred."

The room was deathly quiet. Miss Everett stood still and took a couple of breaths. "Well, the time has come that we can't be ostriches, hiding our heads in the sand. We're caught in the middle of it. Last night in Hines County, the Ku Klux Klan beat a young black man, burned his house down, and possibly raped his wife, and injured his little baby. The facts aren't all clear yet. All I

126

know is that the young man finally, sometime during the night, managed to get some help, and the whole family is, for the moment, safe at the Hines County Hospital."

Miss Everett's eyes were blazing now. "And where are the members of the Ku Klux Klan who did this unspeakable thing? Where indeed? They've melted into shadows, crawled back in the woodwork or, more likely, folded their soiled linen and put away their hoods until the next time. And now they're probably walking around the streets of Hines City like ordinary men."

Without really wanting to, I turned my eyes toward Wanda, trying not to move my head. Her coal black eyes were still, unblinking, and I simply couldn't tell what was going on in her head. I hoped that she didn't know, would never have to know, that her father had been there dressed in one of those sheets.

Miss Everett had lowered her voice. "I've shocked you, and I'm sorry. But maybe I meant to shock you. I know you kids probably didn't have a thing to do with any of this—but kids have a way of growing up, and someday, possibly before you're ready for it, this will be your problem."

Miss Everett sat down in her swivel chair. Very calmly, as though she had used up all her feelings, she said,"I wish this were the end of the horror story, but it isn't. Something else happened in Hines City last night which isn't quite as awful but certainly bad enough. Nobody knows if it was the Klan or not, but vandals went out to Miss Sadie Cohen's house, slashed the tires on her old Cadillac, turned it upside down, and painted swastikas on it and a lot of obscene words." She added, still without expression, "End of story."

Off in the distance, I could hear the courthouse clock striking the hour of ten, and then came the recess bell.

Rising to her feet, Miss Everett said in a normal voice, "Class dismissed—please report to the auditorium when recess is over."

Papa was on the front porch when I got home from school, cleaning a fishing reel. He plopped in a few little drops of 3-in-One oil and screwed the top back on the can. "Hi, Sandy—and how did your day go?"

"OK, I guess," I answered and started to open the screen door.

"Wait up, Sandy, I want to talk with you."

"Papa, I can't—I have to go change my clothes," I said, still hoping to escape. What I really had to do was get down to the swamp and check on Will.

"Your clothes can wait. Here, have a seat." His right hand pointed out the rocker next to his. Gingerly I perched on the very edge, still poised for flight. Papa noticed and spoke more firmly, "You might as well settle back because what I have to say might take a little time."

I narrowed my shoulders and pressed against the cane-backed rocker, willing myself to go deaf. But it didn't work. There was no way to shut out Papa's words. Until we started speaking the same language again I saw no point in talking.

"Sandy—" he was saying, "off and on, all day, I've been thinking about last night and our talk at the breakfast table, and I'm upset about the whole thing. And I gather you're upset. Am I correct?"

"Yes, Papa."

"Can you tell me exactly what it is that's bugging you?"

"No, Papa."

Papa shook his head. "Whatever's wrong, I feel you're blowing it up way out of proportion. You're behaving as though you're angry with the whole darned world, and you're blaming me unfairly. Come off it, Sandy—have I done anything to you?"

"No, Papa."

"For God's sake, Sandy—can't you say anything but 'Yes, Papa,' 'No, Papa'?"

Before I could stop myself, I answered, "No, Papa." Once we both would have laughed at that. Sadly I wondered if we'd ever laugh together again.

I got up from my chair. "May I be excused?"

Just as formally, Papa replied, "You're excused."

Then, one hand on the handle of the door, I turned back around. "I forgot to ask—has Mama come home yet?"

"She came home early this morning. She said she'd busy herself with her family history until we finished our talk—which we apparently have. She's in the dining room."

CHAPTER 15

*M*ama *was practically* hidden behind the stacks of manila folders, loose papers, and metal file boxes that covered the dining room table. Even with a streak of carbon across her cheek and a pencil stuck behind one ear, she looked mighty good to me, in spite of the fact I was scared to face her.

"Hi, Mama—I'm home," I said.

"So am I," she replied, in typical Mama-fashion. "But what a pretty kettle of fish to come home to. I could have died when your father told me what happened last night—the very idea of you and the Dewberry kids pulling a stunt like that. I don't understand you, Sandy. Do you enjoy upsetting me and making me nervous?"

"Of course not, Mama. I'm sorry."

She shook her head and made a clucking noise. "You know, don't you, that you're going to have to be punished for what you did—lying to your father, putting yourself in a dangerous situation like that, and worrying me half to death."

"I said I'm sorry."

"Being sorry doesn't begin to excuse your behavior, Cassandra."

"I guess not," I agreed miserably, "but I am, all the same." After a moment, I added, "Please, Mama, don't be angry with me."

"I'm not angry," she said slowly and not too convincingly, "it's just that I'm terribly disappointed in you." Then, shooing me away with a curt little flip of her fingers, she said, "But run along now—we'll discuss this later. Right now I've got to get back to work." With this, she turned her full attention to all those stacks of family papers on her desk. It was almost as though she was hiding behind them—hiding from me.

I tried to get through to her, "Mama, please let's talk about it now."

She looked at me coldly. "Cassandra, I said we'd discuss this later. Please don't argue with me."

"I'm not arguing with you—how can I argue with you? I don't think you know I'm even alive." All the worry and fear and frustration of the whole long week came boiling up inside me, and suddenly I was pouring out words. "You don't care about me at all. All you care about are those dumb ancestors. Mama, they're dead. They're dead and they're buried and you keep digging them up. That's a crazy thing to do."

"How dare you," Mama said and lurched up from the table, knocking over her papers, scattering Fairchilds and Bigelows in every direction. In slow motion they fluttered down like large white leaves, littering the carpet.

"How dare you?" Mama repeated, as she moved the length of the table and over in my direction.

I wanted to run but I stood my ground, not recognizing my own voice. "But it's true, Mama. You don't care about me—all you care about is a bunch of spooks." And I pointed to the floor where charts and graphs and file cards were a misty blur of squiggly lines. "That's crazy,

Mama, and it's making me hate the Fairchilds—even you!" The words were loud and ugly and I wished I could call them back, but I found myself repeating, "You're making me hate you!"

For the first time in my life, my mother slapped me. A hard, stinging slap. We stood there frozen, staring at each other like total strangers. And this was how Papa found us.

"What in the name of God is going on?" His eyes swept the room and questioned us both. Mama was standing still, her eyes wide with shock and her knuckles pressed against her mouth. I could barely make out her words, but it sounded like she was saying, "Please forgive me, Sandy. You know I didn't mean it."

"It's OK, Mama. I didn't mean it either." I sounded like a wound-up toy, tinny and mechanical.

"What a mess," Papa said, and I don't think he meant just the litter of papers strewn across the floor. He sighed and looked at both of us. "I've got to make a fast trip into town and wondered if either of you might like to go along. Or do you need anything?"

"No, thank you," Mama and I replied in a skinny little chorus.

"Well, in that case, I'll be getting along." Turning back from the door, he added, "It might be a good idea for both of you to get some rest. After all, tonight's the big night, and we'll all need our strength to get Sandy through her speech." With that he went out and Mama and I were left alone, still staring at each other. The color was coming back in Mama's face and she spoke to me in a much more normal voice. "Please, forgive me, Sandy. I promise never to strike you again. As long as I live."

Woodenly, I answered, "It's OK, Mama. Forget it."

132

Mama stooped down to gather up the scattered papers and I hurried to the kitchen.

The sound of Papa's car died away in the distance as I slapped sandwiches together like a short-order cook. I threw them in a bag on top of a can of Coke. Then for added measure I cut a huge wedge of caramel cake, cussing the plastic wrap, which was sticking to all ten fingers. I was glad I had something handy to cuss at. In spite of the apologies that Mama and I had exchanged, I still felt all knotted up inside and angry with the world.

Will answered my whistle immediately and I clambered up the stairs. He motioned for me to sit so I sat, cross-legged, on that skimpy make-believe bed, the moss all dried and squashed down now.

"Sandy, I've got to tell you something."

Suddenly I knew I didn't want to hear whatever he planned to say. It couldn't be good—not with that serious look in his eyes, not with that scary tone in his voice. "Not now. Tell me when you've eaten. I brought ham and cheese and caramel cake—"

Will stopped me with his held-up hand. "Hey, slow down. I'll get to the food. What I have to say won't take but a minute."

I braced myself and waited.

"Sandy, what I'm trying to tell you is that I won't be here tomorrow. I'm leaving tonight."

"But, Will, you can't do that—you plain can't leave tonight. It isn't safe. It really isn't safe."

Will leaned his shoulders against the crooked wall and lifted his head to stare through those crazy splintery cracks that let shiny slivers of daylight through. Then wearily he looked back where I sat. "I know it isn't safe. It probably wouldn't be safe a year from now, but I've got to chance

133

it. My leg is almost healed and I've made up my mind. I've got to go." Turning again, he peered through the tiny window. "I can't stay on here, shut up, for the rest of my life. It seems I've been here for a lifetime."

I let my chin sink down in the cupped palm of my hand. "I know, Will. I know what you're saying and I think I know how you're feeling—but if you'd only wait just one more day. Please."

Will shook his head. "I can't. I've got to get out of here."

I let out a sigh. "I guess your Uncle Pete must have known you were planning to leave. He sent you something today." Reaching down in my pocket, I pulled out the dollar bills, even more wrinkled and wilted. "Here."

Will reached out and, without counting it, transferred the bills to his pocket. "I would have made it without him doing that, but it sure will come in handy." He looked at me with a long, peculiar look and finally said in a serious voice, "Sandy, don't be stubborn—you know the time has come for me to be movin' on—it's long overdue."

"And what if you run right smack into that posse? They're still out there, you know."

"I know." He jerked his head in the direction of the radio. "And from what little scraps of information they're letting out about what happened last night—which isn't much, I grant you; they're trying to hush it up—all of Hines County must be sitting on top of a powder keg."

I tried to reason with him. "Maybe tonight at Commencement I can find out something. Maybe somebody will give a clue where the posse is searching now—which part of the county, at least."

"What if you don't find out a thing? Then what?"

"I'll think of something else," I said, hoping I sounded a lot more confident than I felt.

"OK, OK," Will said, throwing out his hands, looking cornered. He also looked angry with me, but I wouldn't mind how he felt if he'd just stay put for one more night. But, on second thought, I didn't want to leave him angry. Standing up, I walked over to him and gave his check a quick little good-bye kiss. "Well, now that's settled, I'll see you in the morning." From the top of the steps, I shook my finger at him. "Promise me that you won't change your mind after I'm gone."

Will gave me a grin. "I promise. I wouldn't dare. I wouldn't put it past you, Sandy Cason, to come hotfooting after me and drag me back by the nape of the neck."

My sneakers skidded along the dead-weed path which, in just this week, I'd worn down slick and smooth. If the posse ever started at my kitchen door, this path would lead as straight as a plumb bob on a string to Will in the tree house. For that matter, if Papa or Mama took a notion to wander down to the swamp, this path would lead to disaster. Will was right—he had to go. It might not be safe to go, but it wasn't safe to stay. He had to take a long shot, and I had to make myself believe it would work. He had to get away safely over the border, and he had to do it tomorrow.

The empty space in the garage meant that Papa was still not back from Hines City. Softly I walked past the dining room door through which I could see Mama still sitting at the table, which was bare and empty now except for the satin glass bowl in the center. In spite of myself I paused and looked at Mama who, as far as I could tell, wasn't doing anything but staring off into space.

135

I started to move on when suddenly Mama looked at me and said across the distance, "Oh, there you are. Where on earth have you been?"

Through habit, I gave her the usual answer, "Nowhere, Mama. Just around." My ears were popping with my effort not to cry.

The three of us sat at the table, pushing the simple supper around on our plates, not eating, just marking time. We were already dressed for Commencement—Papa with a white-on-white shirt, Mama with her pink linen sheath, and me, decked out in the white dotted swiss Mama and I had bought on one of our last shopping trips. We sat stiffly in our places like brand-new paper dolls, cutouts of a family folded at the middle, propped there at the table. Anyone watching us might have thought that the most important thing in the world was that we didn't start sagging or get all rumpled and mussed up.

From his end of the table, Papa cleared his throat but he didn't say anything. Mama and I weren't even trying to talk. We didn't even look at each other. In all this silence, I was beginning to feel like a rubber band stretched beyond the giving point, ready to *zing* and let go. Pushing away from the table, I addressed a spot above Mama's head, "May I please be excused?"

I don't think Mama even heard me, but Papa said, "Wait just a minute, Sandy." Reaching into his pocket, he pulled out a little wrapped-up box and laid it by my plate. I sat there staring at it and Papa slid it closer to my hand. "Go on, open it up. It's just a little something your mother and I wanted you to have to celebrate your Commencement."

I eased open the white gift paper and slipped out the jeweler's box. Inside, nestled in satin, was a gold charm bracelet, and on the heart-shaped charm was engraved in tiny letters, *Cassandra Cason, May 1965. With love from Mama and Papa.*

I managed to stammer, "Thank you. Thank you both very much. It's beautiful."

It *was* beautiful. And yet the charm bracelet felt awfully cold and fragile in my hand. I measured it around my wrist and Mama, who had risen from the table, fastened the safety catch with fingers that trembled a little.

My parents looked at me. Their faces had lost that paper doll look and they were real again, animated with love—but they didn't try to touch me. And I didn't reach out to them. All of us knew it wasn't that simple or easy. To knit this family back together again would take time, maybe a lot of time.

We were quiet as riverbed stones all the way to town. Goodness only knows what Mama and Papa were thinking, but all I could hear in my head were the words of the Gettysburg Address, jumbled up together, making no sense at all. And I was convincing myself that by the time we reached the auditorium, I would have total amnesia.

It was early, but when we parked there were people milling around all over the place. Remembering my promise to Will to gather any information I could, I looked for posse members. A few of them were there, but tonight they were being fathers, ordinary fathers—clean-shaven, hair slicked down, and tugging at their unaccustomed ties—beaming with pride, reaching out to their children to flick off a piece of lint or smooth down a cowlick.

My parents had drifted away to speak to friends and

Wanda and Roy Lee walked over to where I stood. Roy Lee looked strange without his baseball cap, but his voice was as soft and easy as ever, "Good luck, Sandy, with your speech." He closed one eye in a wink and circled his thumb and finger in the go ahead sign.

Wanda, reading my mind as usual, said, "You're right —that brother of mine is coming out of his shell in a great big way." Then cocking her head to one side she surveyed me tip to toe. "I guess you'll do,"she decided, "but it's been weeks since we cut your hair and it's growing like wildfire. I think we ought to give you one of those new body waves."

Protecting my head with both hands, I shrieked, "Not on your life. Before I'd let you get near my hair again, I'd pull it out at the roots, strand by strand."

Wanda grinned. "I don't blame you, Sandy. I really did butcher you." Before wandering off in search of boys she looked at me, dark eyes full of mischief and, for a moment, she was exactly the Wanda I used to know. "I'll call you later, Sandy. I've dreamed up a bunch of things for us to do to get through the summer."

Inside, I had my stage fright before I even reached the stage. I found my place, third chair from the center, and when the program started I listened to the introduction but not to the speeches that followed. Through all those days of practice, I'd memorized them all, but now they were just a bee-droning buzz of meaningless sound. Although my body sat there, dressed in dotted swiss, vacant-faced, pretending, I let my mind drift away from the scene.

My turn had come. I took a breath and held it while Miss Everett stepped forward and said something which ended with, "the Gettysburg Address by Cassandra Cason."

Cassandra. So formal. It didn't sound like me. I didn't feel like me. Even my voice wasn't mine when I began. But even before I reached the end of that long first sentence—*all men are created equal*—I knew that I would make it. I was doing fine.

I didn't rush the ending. The words came out easily, loud and clear: *and that government of the people, by the people, for the people, shall not perish from the earth.*

I vaguely saw Miss Everett's proud and loving smile; I scarcely heard the clapping when I sat back down. All I knew for sure was that Commencement was over.

CHAPTER 16

*M*y *parents let* me sleep through breakfast the following morning. I was still in bed playing possum when they came in my room.

Papa shook my shoulder, real easy. "Hey, Tom-girl, come back to the land of the living. We're going shopping in Hines City. You want to go, or would last night's star performer prefer her beauty sleep?"

Mama considered that for a moment. "I never have been convinced that extra sleep would make a person pretty."

Papa laughed. "Well, don't fret about it, Laura. The way you look today, you don't need any beauty aids."

It was true, Mama did look pretty in her green pantsuit and should have been going somewhere special instead of the grocery store.

Almost as though she read my thoughts, Mama said, "But if we don't go to the grocery store, we're going to starve. I've got a list as long as my arm. We're out of everything—the grits has weevils in it, we're getting short on shortening, and we're right down to that very last drop of Maxwell House coffee."

Things were looking brighter. Mama was making jokes again, or trying to. Maybe trying *too* hard, but at least it was a beginning. I laughed, and Papa leaned over and gave me a kiss, and unexpectedly, so did Mama.

When the sound of their car died away, I dressed and hurried to the kitchen, where I fixed a larger than usual lunch for Will. I had no way of telling just how long it would take him to get across the border and down to Mayport in Florida. I had a sad, empty feeling, knowing the time had almost come to say good-bye to Will.

I gave our special whistle, and when Will whistled back I went tearing up the steps. As soon as I was inside, Will asked, "Did you find out anything last night about the posse?"

"Not much," I admitted. "All I know is that they're still out there looking for you. But I've been doing some thinking. I've decided you're right about leaving. We've been lucky so far, but I've got an awful hunch our luck is running out."

"You and me both." Will looked around the room. "Gosh, Sandy, I'm leaving this place a bloody wreck. It'll take a two-ton truck to haul away all this stuff." One corner was completely taken up with empty bottles, cans, the radio, the hammer, flashlight, and other things I'd smuggled in for him.

"That's OK, don't worry about it. I got it all down here, so I'm sure I can get it all back, a little bit at a time. Now that school's out, I'll have a lot of time on my hands."

"Speaking of school, how did things go last night with your speech?"

"Fine, I guess. At least it's over with." We sat quietly for a long moment, then I asked, "Will, have you figured out the best time for you to leave?"

"I don't know exactly, but I think I better wait until it gets good and dark." He reached for the radio and turned it on real low. "Let's listen to the news, and maybe we can get a weather report."

We waited through a country western song and a batch of commercials. Neither of us cared that Thig's Pig was opening another barbecue place on Highway 309 or that the Downtown Gulf was offering a free car wash with a fill-up. Suddenly Will leaned forward, turned off the radio, and made a shushing gesture. "Listen," he whispered.

As plain as anything, we could hear people walking heavily through the brush—the crackle of leaves and twigs being trampled underfoot, and voices, loud and careless. Whoever was approaching the tree house made no effort to keep down the noise.

I was on the side nearest the little window, so I eased myself close against the wall and raised my eyes quickly to peer outside. I ducked back down and stared at Will, saying in the lowest possible voice, "It's Lester O'Kelly and Pearl."

They were coming closer and closer and were almost under the tree. There wasn't any way to mistake Lester's braying laugh, and his words were loud and clear. "Aw come on, Pearl—why you scared to go up in that little house with me?"

"It ain't that I'm scared, Lester O'Kelly—I just got better sense."

"Than what?"

"Than to let you corner me anywhere." She giggled, and after a pause she added coaxingly, "Here, come get a drink of water from this flowing well. Maybe it'll cool you down a tad."

"Not me," Lester snorted. "I can't stand artesian water —too much sulphur in it. Smells like rotten eggs."

Pearl squealed. "Well, suit yourself, but let me alone so I can get a drink."

"You ain't all that thirsty—you just playin' for time."

Will and I had each found a crack big enough to see through without being seen from below, and wordlessly we watched the couple horsing around. Pearl was squealing and spluttering with good reason, since Lester was bobbing her head up and down in the trough like a Halloween apple. Each time she surfaced, she yelled a little louder, "Come on, Lester. Hey, cut it out. You've ruined my hair."

He had. Her hair was a wet stringy mop and her cotton blouse was soaked, plastered to her chest, making her look like a topless go-go girl.

Then Lester pushed her head down in the trough, completely underwater, and when she finally managed to jerk it up she screamed, "What do you think you're doin'? Have you gone crazy?"

"Take it easy, baby, I was just funnin' around."

"That ain't fun. You can drown a person that way." She was shivering and shaking all over.

"Aw, be a sport, Pearl," said Lester, who had flopped down on the ground. "Come on over here and let me warm you up."

"Not me. I'm goin' home. And you can go to blazes." It sounded as though her teeth were chattering. She stood there, glaring down at Lester, trying to wring the water from her dripping blouse. "I really mean it, Lester—I'm freezin' and I'm goin' home."

"Go on, then. I ain't beggin' nobody," drawled Lester, who had stretched out full length and was chewing on a blade of grass. "You ain't the only fish in the sea."

"Yeah, I know, you're a regular ladies' man. Only trouble is, you haven't got the foggiest notion of how to treat a lady."

"How would you know? You sure as hell don't qualify as a lady." Lester sat up. "What you are is a tease—you promise, but you don't deliver."

"Well, if you don't like the way I act, go on back to your other girls. Go back to that married woman you used to tell me about."

"What married woman, Pearl?" Lester's words were carefully measured. "I ain't said nothin' to you about no married woman."

"Sure you did. You used to brag all the time how it was with her. How crazy she was about you."

Lester got to his feet and moved toward Pearl, standing very close, and his tone was threatening. "Let's get somethin' straight right now, there ain't no married woman and there never was."

Pearl stepped back a couple of steps. "Sure, Lester. Forget I said it. I didn't mean to make you so mad. After all, if we're going to part, we can still part friends." Sounding like one of the pages of her *True Confessions*, she added dramatically, "You can keep my photograph I gave you, and the red silk scarf." She paused and looked at Lester. "But tell me something—why have you quit wearin' the scarf? For a while, you wore it every day."

"What scarf? Pearl, you're out of your ever lovin' mind. You ain't never given me a scarf." Now his voice was really ugly and menacing.

That did it. Pearl might be a lot of things—loud-mouthed and boy-crazy—but she can add two and two. And so could the two of us in the tree house. We could feel it coming. We could almost tell what was going to happen next.

Pearl stood stock-still, arms across her chest, staring

144

Lester down. They were directly below us, and the tree house wasn't very far off the ground, so we could hear every word. Pearl's voice was suprisingly steady and controlled. "Lester O'Kelly, it was you. You strangled that woman in Hines City."

"Pearl, like I said, you're crazy, really out of your gourd." He reached out a hand to touch her but Pearl backed away.

"Yeah, I agree, I'm crazy—I'm crazy for not seein' it sooner. I should have known from the beginning that it was you who killed that woman, strangled her to death with the red silk scarf I gave you." She was rapidly losing control, and her words were slipping and sliding up and down the scale. "I know you, Lester, and I knew that somethin' was really buggin' you. But I didn't think, I didn't even dream—" Her voice broke and she stood there, flapping her hands in the air.

"Well, Miss Smarty, now that you think you got the whole thing figured out, what are you plannin' to do?" Lester inched closer, clenching his fists, rubbing them on his jeans.

"I don't know—I've got to do some thinkin'—"

"You do that," Lester snarled, "but let me tell you a thing or two—you breathe a word of what you're thinkin', and I double guarantee you, you've breathed your last. You hear?"

"I hear. I won't tell. I won't," Pearl promised, taking two or three uncertain steps backward. "Cross my heart, I won't." Still edging away from him, she was getting ready to run. I could sense it. So could Lester.

Through the twisted sneer of his mouth, Lester said, "On second thought, if I let you go, you might stir up a lot of grief for me—and I can't have that." Snaking out his arm, he grabbed her wrist. Frantically, Pearl was trying to work free. Each time she pulled away, Lester got madder and madder. He reached out for her throat.

Inside the tree house, we stared disbelievingly for a brief moment and then Will whispered, "There's gonna be big trouble. I'm going down." He hobbled to the door, with me right behind him. We reached the ground just as Lester had tightened his hands around Pearl's throat and was clamping down with all his strength.

Will lunged at Lester and tackled him to the ground. Lester lay stunned and surprised for a couple of seconds, staring up at us. He started scrambling up, seizing on Will's bad leg, and the next thing I knew, Pearl grabbed the heavy claw hammer out of my hand—I hadn't even known I had brought it down—and she gave old Lester a solid whack on the side of his head, and he fell back on the ground with a thud. Then Pearl and Will divided Lester up and sat all over him. Lester blinked his eyes, stopped heaving and struggling, and lay there. He was whimpering a little and panting a lot, but so far saying nothing.

"Run, Sandy," Will commanded. "Go get your daddy."

I took off, looking over my shoulder. The two of them had Lester pinned to the ground for now, but even though Will is awfully big and strong, how long could they hold him?

I've spent a lot of my time running somewhere or other, but never with such desperation. Skidding to a stop at my back door, I could tell at a glance that Papa and Mama had not come back from town. I felt like screaming.

Racing to the kitchen phone, I dialed the operator. "Please," I said, "ring the sheriff's office." I could hear it ringing while I rocked from side to side waiting impatiently for what seemed forever.

Finally a voice drawled, "Sheriff Wiggins here."

I practically yelled at him, "Sheriff, this is Sandy Cason. Bring some men and come out here as fast as you can."

"Whoa, young lady—not so fast. Tell me again who this is."

"Sandy Cason—Tom Cason's daughter. Please hurry up and come."

"Now I know who you are. What seems to be your trouble?"

"I'll tell you when you get here," I said, rudely banging down the phone.

I was stuck. I couldn't leave before the sheriff arrived, or Mama and Papa, or somebody. Lord, just anybody. I had to hold myself down to keep from running off back to the swamp. I couldn't stand not knowing what was going on down there.

Turning to the phone again, I dialed the Dewberrys' number, sure I'd have a flipping fit if I got one of the Gruesome Twosome. This time I was lucky. What a relief to hear Roy Lee's quiet voice say hello.

"Roy Lee, this is Sandy. Are your parents home?"

"As far as I know—at least they were a little while ago."

I swallowed, not sure what to say next. Roy Lee prompted, "Why?"

I swallowed again and managed to stammer, "It's Pearl. She's down in the swamp behind our house and she's in trouble. I think y'all better come get her. In a hurry."

Without a good-bye, I laid the phone back in its cradle and rested my head for a moment against the kitchen wall. And then I heard it, growing louder and louder— the wail of the sheriff's siren.

Sprinting to the front of the hosue, I saw that Mama

147

and Papa were pulling up in the driveway behind the sheriff's car. They were all piling out of the cars, and the sheriff and two of his men were questioning Papa. But all he did was shake his head and hold up his hands in a bewildered way. Barreling down from the porch, I ran to Papa, wedging myself in between him and the sheriff and saying to both of them, "Come—come on." Taking Papa's hand, I started tugging in the direction of the swamp.

Mama's voice called out, "Cassandra. What is this all about?"

"I can't tell you now. Come on, Papa, hurry—we've got to get to the tree house."

Mama started to follow and I waved her back, "No, Mama, please. The Dewberrys are coming—you better wait for them."

I didn't even look to see if the sheriff and his men were keeping up. Still holding Papa's hand, I literally pulled him around the house, and then because that narrow path is better single file, I led the way, with all the men just tagging along behind me. I could hear the sheriff puffing and snorting, and his keys and handcuffs were jingling with every step.

Papa outdistanced me and yanked me to a stop. "Cassandra," he said, using Mama's name for me, "Cassandra, before we go another inch, you've got some explaining to do."

Papa and Sheriff Wiggins and his deputies—all four men—stood there in a knot, stock-still, waiting for an answer.

As fast as I could, tripping over my words, I tried—I really tried—to get through to them. "You've all been out there looking for Will Brown—but Will didn't kill that woman. Lester O'Kelly did it. And he tried to strangle

Pearl Dewberry. And Pearl and Will are holding Lester—I *hope* they're still holding Lester—and we've got to hurry." Tugging at Papa again, I said, "Come on—come on."

Papa held up his hand. "One last question. Am I correct in my impression that boy has been hiding on our property for a week—with your help?"

"Papa, I had to help him. He was hurt—but, please, let's talk about that later. We've got to go."

The men were looking at me as though I'd gone mad, and I couldn't blame them. Dancing up and down, I shouted, "Hurry—oh, please hurry—"

Papa gave me a baffled, searching look I won't ever forget, but all he said was, "Lead on." Now the men set out a little faster, widening the path, two and three abreast, bending the mullein and dog fennel and gallberry bushes under their heavy boots. I could smell the greenish bitter smell of freshly crushed verbena.

We reached the tree house clearing in record time, and there they were—just as I'd left them—Will straddling Lester's shoulders and Pearl across Lester's legs, still holding that old claw hammer in her hand. The fight had gone out of Lester. His eyes were still glazed from the blow on his head, and he had a stupid, sullen look.

The men took over. It was good to have Will, and even Pearl, crowding close around me. We watched as the sheriff leaned over, collaring Lester and yanking him to his feet. Lester stood up, trying to bluff his way out, while the sheriff mumbled something about his right to remain silent. But, when the handcuffs snapped into place, Lester suddenly wilted. With one last blustering attempt, he said, "Hey, man, you makin' a big mistake."

"Maybe so," drawled the sheriff, "but somehow I doubt it." Then turning to Will, he said, "As for you, boy, don't you be leavin' town just yet. You still got a mite of explainin' to do before we get to the bottom of this mess."

"Yes sir," was Will's reply. None of us said another word while the men led Lester O'Kelly, head hanging, shrunken looking, up the path.

Sheriff Wiggins called back over his shoulder, "You comin', Tom?"

Papa replied, "Not right this minute, Sheriff. I'll talk to you when you get back to town."

"Sure thing," the sheriff said and kept on walking.

Papa laid his arm around my shoulder and all of us stood still and silent as the men tramped out of sight, bending and breaking more of the weeds on either side.

Finally I turned to Papa. "Many more trips like this, and we'll have a regular road to my tree house instead of a path."

Papa gave a short little laugh. "Let's pray there won't ever be another trip like this." Looking over to Will, he asked, "Are you all right? This must have been quite an ordeal for you."

"I'm OK," Will replied. "I banged up my leg a little more during the scuffle with Lester, but I can manage."

"Here," Papa said, "lean part of your weight on me and let's head back for the house." Together they started out—Papa, sure and strong, and Will, limping and hobbling along, fielding Papa's questions. I was glad that Will would have this chance to do some of the answering before my turn came, but I knew my time was coming.

I glanced over at Pearl. I've never seen anyone quite so bedraggled. Her hair, still damp, was matted and tangled, her shirt was streaked and wrinkled, and she'd picked up a couple of nasty scratches on her face, which was white as a sheet. But the strangest thing about Pearl

150

—she wasn't talking. I've never known Pearl when she didn't have something to say.

I reached out my hand. "Pearl, are you all right?"

She didn't answer. Her eyes got wider and wider and her face had taken on a blotchy look. But then she blinked, focused her eyes, and said, "That so-and-so was really goin' to kill me."

Pearl, now that she'd found her voice, would probably be OK, so I suggested, "Hey, let's go," and both of us moved at a decent speed back to our house.

Our backyard was filled with a lot of people, all staring in our directon. The sheriff's car was gone, thank goodness, but everybody else was there, including Mr. Wall-Eye. Where on earth had he come from?

With a wave in the general direction of Wanda and Roy Lee, I walked over to Mama who had been cornered by Mrs. Dewberry. Mama said politely, "Excuse me, Sal," and held out her arms to me in a loving half circle. For one who isn't practiced at hugging and kissing, she did a super job.

Together we watched as Pearl went up to her family. To my surprise—I don't know why exactly—it was Mr. Dewberry that Pearl walked up to first. Mr. Dewberry, the quiet shadow who never says anything, was the one who held out his arms for Pearl. And Pearl—grown-up, overgrown, boy-crazy, and all—laid her head on her father's shoulder and cried like a baby.

Will had limped over and was standing close to me and Mama. "Mama," I said, "you remember Will Brown?"

"Of course," said Mama, in her most ladylike manner, "I remember Will Brown. I'm glad to see you, Will." And she held out her hand. "I not only remember Will, I remember his mother and his grandmother." She repeated, "I'm glad to see you, Will."

"Same here," Will said. "Mrs. Cason, I'm fixing to leave. Could I speak to Sandy before I go?"

"Certainly, Will," said Mama, still gracious. "Besides, I ought to check on my other guests."

I followed Will over to the side of the turkey pen. "Will," I said, "you'll just have to overlook Mama. That's just Mama's way, pretending this is a party."

Will smiled. "I don't mind. For me it is a party, a coming out party."

"To me it looks more like a family reunion."

"Girl, you're off your rocker," Will teased. "They might be integrating the schools and the buses, but there ain't no way they're integrating families in Hines County, Georgia. No way."

I tried not to laugh. If I started laughing now, I wouldn't know how to stop. We walked to the far edge of the backyard. "Here, sit down for just a minute before you leave," I said, pointing out the old abandoned wash bench. Once we were seated I turned to Will and asked, "Now that it's over, what are you planning to do?"

"I don't really know. I've thought about it, what I'd do if again I had a choice. I had plenty of thinking time down there in the tree house all by myself. And I decided, first off, that I wouldn't go to Florida. I'd get seasick and I'd be a terrible shrimper. I'll wait and go to Florida as an ordinary tourist."

"Well, what then—?"

"I can't do anything, of course, until the trial is over. You heard what the sheriff said. But once it is, I might go up to Alabama and look for my sister Hessie. And, after that, who knows—maybe I'll go over and help old Benjie fight his war."

"That would be just nifty," I exploded. "I can see me going through life plastered to the front page of the paper

152

and glued to the TV set, trying to get the news from all over the world. Worrying about Selma and Montgomery and Vietnam. Worrying my head off." I meant it as a sort of joke, but it didn't come out that way. It was far too true and scary. Trying to change the subject, I asked, "What are you going to do about your high school diploma?"

Sounding bitter, Will said, "They can keep it or they can make confetti of it—I couldn't care less." After a moment, he added, "They've had Commencement without me, so it really doesn't matter. I don't need the formalities, I've graduated without them."

"I know," I persisted. "But I wish you'd remember what I told you that Miss Everett said—commencement has two meanings. It isn't just an ending—it's a beginning. Maybe your commencement is still going on."

Will reached over and gave my hair a tweak. "Sandy, you're something else. Really something."

He got to his feet, wincing a little as he put his weight down on his bad leg. "Sandy, I've got to go. It's time to say good-bye."

I tried to make my voice casual. "I don't like good-byes. Do you mind if I just say, I'll see you later?"

Will stood there for a moment, looking down at me. "Sandy," he said, giving me that crooked smile, "I want you to know"—he was struggling for words like I do all the time—"that I'll carry this week, and you, like a good luck charm—like a lucky rabbit's foot—for the rest of my life."

We were saying good-bye and both of us knew it, whether we liked it or not. Sure, maybe we'd see each other around—someplace, sometime—but this was good-bye.

I sat there on the rickety wooden bench and watched him walk away from me, growing smaller and smaller.

153

He could no longer hear me, but softly I said, "Good-bye, Will."

He was cutting through the empty fields where he and Benjie had walked side by side after their hunting trips. Squeezing my eyes together, I felt like a little kid again and I could almost see the two of them, shotguns angled over their shoulders, knapsacks filled with small game, occasionally reaching out, straight-arming each other, sharing some secret joke. They moved through the edges of my memory like shadowy figures in a dream, and it was hard to believe they'd ever really existed. My heart told me that I'd lost Benjie years ago, long before he joined the navy and traveled to the far side of the globe. And now, today, I was losing Will. He too was disappearing from my world.

Opening my eyes, I could feel the tears slipping out, rolling down the sides of my face, making a salty film. Angrily, with the heel of my hand, I brushed them away and looked off in the distance. No way would I allow my very last vision of Will Brown to be all blurred and fuzzy. I wanted to see him clearly—not just for now but for the rest of my life.

About the Author

Beth Bland Engel was born in south Georgia, and has lived in North Carolina, Alabama, Tennessee, Florida, and Louisiana. Her young adult novel, *Ride the Pine Sapling*, has been nominated for the Georgia Children's Book Award. And her adult book, *The Middleton Family*, won the Donald Lines Jacobus Award from the National Society of Genealogy.

Big Words is based on two stories—"The Knife," which received the Anne Flexner Memorial Award at Duke University, and "Big Words," which won an Alabama Arts Festival Award in 1978.

Ms. Engel has two daughters and now lives in Brunswick, Georgia.